# THINKING ABOUT EUROPE

# THINKING ABOUT EUROPE

Roger Woodhouse

Thumbnail Publications

Published in Great Britain by
Thumbnail Publications
Sutton Coldfield

ISBN  0-9550223-0-4

Printed and bound in Great Britain by
Lamberts Print & Design
Settle, North Yorkshire

# CONTENTS

1: THE EUROPEAN PROJECT

More Questions than Answers          1
In the Beginning                     2
Method and Machinery                 8
The Three Frenchmen                  9


2: WHEELS WITHIN WHEELS

Law and Order                       13
The European Commission             14
The Council of Ministers            17
The European Parliament             19
Regulations and Directives          28


3: FLIES IN THE OINTMENT

The Common Agricultural Policy      33
The Euro                            37
Defence Policy                      42


4: THE GHOST IN THE MACHINE

Ever Closer Union                   51
Theory and Practice                 60
The European Mind                   66


5: EUROPE FOR EVERYONE

Convention and Constitution         73
The Day after Tomorrow              78

# 1: THE EUROPEAN PROJECT

## More Questions than Answers

What is the European Union all about? What does it mean? Where is it going?

When these questions are raised, the barrage of conflicting answers can give the impression that the whole subject is best left to the experts. On the other hand, anything that affects our lives is our business. That is democracy, and to make it work everyone must have some idea of what is going on. How difficult can that be? Basically we only need to know two things:

1) What does the European Union **do**?
2) What is the European Union **for**?

But the very fact that the question comes in two halves gives a hint of the real problem. If there was a simple answer to part two, the functions of the EU could be judged accordingly, but because the final purpose and the full scope of European integration have never been agreed, it is difficult to say if the European Union is doing the right things or heading in the right direction. The EU is well established as an administrative framework within which decisions are taken and rules made, but the human values that underpin it, the beliefs that sustain it and the destiny to which it might legitimately aspire remain subjects for debate.

If the process of European integration had a clear end point, the cases for and against could be considered on their merits and the project then either abandoned or taken to its final stage. As things stand, Europe has been under construction for half a century and the question of **why** has always been fudged, while the question of **how** has been dealt with according to circumstances. Europe has thus developed the means to do what it does while the whole object of the exercise remains open to interpretation.

For some, an integrated Europe is primarily good commercial sense based on open frontiers and fair competition. For others, this is only the first stage in the growth of a unified Europe which will eventually embrace, absorb or supersede the political attributes of the member countries as sovereign states. Over the years these contrasting views have been accommodated within the same design by deliberate vagueness in the wording of the documents that provide the legal basis for the Europe under

*1*

construction. It would be simpler if the objective had been fixed once and for all: either a common market or a superstate. Metaphorically speaking, the foundations were laid and work started before deciding if the contract was for a general store or a civic centre. This makes it hard to tell if the doors and windows are in the right place or if the walls are strong enough.

Without pushing the analogy too far, it can be seen that a casual visitor might look round such a building site without him or her being any the wiser. This is exactly the position of the average citizen when contemplating the European Union. If the outsider cannot make head nor tail of it at first glance it is not at all surprising. The EU is the brainchild of many fathers and a continuing experiment on a huge scale. Any attempt to assign a meaning to the whole enterprise has to explain both the form that it takes and the ideas that it is supposed to embody. Because some of those ideas go back centuries and some are relatively recent developments, the full picture requires a long perspective. This means taking a plunge into the deep end of European history.

## In the Beginning

With the fall of the Roman Empire in western Europe in 410 AD, the region degenerated into strife and confusion as warlike tribes from the east moved in. Within a few years, however, the spread of the Christian religion began to give a fresh coherence to life and society in the lands once ruled by the Caesars. In the year 498, Clovis became the first barbarian to be baptised and rule as a Christian king. He and other leaders who followed his example learned seamlessly to combine their interests with those of the Church and in so doing brought an extra dimension to the pattern of loyalty and duty which defined relations with their subjects.

Soon, however, a new power based on religion rose in the shape of Islam. By 710, Moslem armies had crossed the Mediterranean, conquered Spain and moved into France. This tide was stemmed decisively in 732 at the battle of Tours with the victory of the army of Charles Martel. With his death in 741 the succession of his son was not assured but Pippin the Short took the throne with the blessing of the Pope, who had him anointed in a solemn ceremony and called upon the faithful to obey their leader as a religious obligation. This support changed the very nature of kingship; henceforth the monarch ruled not according to custom and practice but 'by the grace of God'.

In his reign, Pippin's son, Charlemagne, established a Christian empire covering large parts of present day Germany, France and Italy. From this beginning, Europe of the Middle Ages became synonymous with Christendom. All across this area, the life of the commoner was bound by a double duty to monarch and Church stretching down through the aristocracy on one hand and the ranks of the priesthood on the other. In every country, the king's men enforced his law while throughout Europe as a whole, churches and monasteries spread a network of religious observance which underpinned the secular power of the throne. From Avignon in the south of France to Rievaulx Abbey in Yorkshire, the Church's men worked, travelled and communicated in a vast undertaking which went beyond the spiritual into the realms of politics and economics. The effect was something like the influence that multinational corporations exert over governments today: a management of mutual interests which shaped the everyday world. Moreover, with faith supporting duty, everyone knew his or her place in the scheme of things in a way which had no need of national sentiment to complete the picture.

It was not just the rise of scientific rationalism or the emergence of Protestantism that called into question this view of the world. It was the crowned heads of Europe themselves who began to see advantages in drawing legitimacy more from their traditional sovereignty over a territory than the less certain backing of the Church. For peasant and noble alike it was the now the land beneath their feet rather than the heaven above that made them what they were. As nation and state became inextricably entwined, the confined space of western Europe was beset by rivalries as the relation of the individual to the whole was increasingly understood in terms of the needs of king and country.

The centuries passed and the peace was regularly shattered as great armies contended for possession of this or that muddy field. While such things were decided by leadership, courage and whatever material could be dragged along by a horse, it was at least a time-honoured sort of bloodshed. The banners waved, the bugles blew, the heroes charged and those back at home waited for the news.

Everything changed with the industrial revolution. The resources in money and materials demanded by an economy based on expanding production of manufactured goods engendered more bitter rivalries and a different sort of war for which the factories turned out new weapons of ever greater power. In 1870, France lost a war with Prussia because the latter was better prepared industrially. Henceforth, wars would be fought between machines with the frail bodies of men acting only as counters on the scoreboard.

The Great War of 1914-18 took this logic to the limit for its time and was called the 'War to end all wars'. With the lesson apparently learned, the

League of Nations seemed for a while to offer hope that world peace could be founded on international arbitration and conciliation. However, as Europe was the potential hotspot for renewed conflict, there were some who turned their minds towards what was clearly the heart of the problem. If war sprang from a combination of rampant nationalism and unrestrained industrialisation, there were two possible ways to defuse the situation:

1) Change the way nations thought about each other,
2) Put industry across Europe on some sort of co-operative basis.

For the sake of labelling, we might call the proponents of a human, spiritual approach 'Dreamers', and those who sought an industrial and economic solution 'Technicians'. The methods favoured were different but from both points of view it was obvious that action on an effective scale could not fail to have a political effect.

The leading light of the 'Dreamers' was Count Coudenhove-Kalergi, an Austrian nobleman who formed the Pan-European Union to spread the doctrine that the key to peace and prosperity was a federation based on the defining characteristics of European civilization:

1) The value of the individual: the idea that it is right for people to be themselves, to seek their own intellectual and personal development.
2) The social and humanitarian traits of the Christian religion: inclusiveness and sympathy for one's fellows.
3) The principles of chivalry: the code of knights of old who combined heroism with decency and generosity.

The goal was therefore not merely a political and economic community but a homeland for the European soul: the homeland of pride, love and honour.

The appeal of the Pan-European Union was thus to a large extent based on nostalgia for the days when Europe was synonymous with Christendom. It did, therefore, suffer from a sort of residual elitism. When the bishop in his cathedral conversed in Latin with the knight in his armour, their common cultural space was not open to the peasant in his hovel. All the same, the legacy of those days is still a vague impression that a Europe for everyone already exists but has, in a sense, been mislaid and can be found again, or is asleep and needs only to be awakened.

This is a vision which even now retains the power to inspire but has in fact been rather out of step with political reality since Edmund Burke lamented in the aftermath of the French Revolution: 'But the age of chivalry is gone. That of sophisters, economists, and calculators has succeeded; and the glory of Europe is extinguished for ever.' Forty years before the first railway, Burke was thus already mourning the passing of a Europe founded on piety and gentlemanly conduct. That was also, moreover, a Europe in which privilege and religion were the warp and weft of a society in which everyone knew his place. Aspects of this lost world may still exert a certain charm but their appeal is far from universal and they cannot be said to reflect in a general sense how Europeans think about themselves as a group.

This is even more true today than it was in the 1920s, when the first of the 'Technicians', the French socialist Aristide Briand, began to see Europe in more modern terms. The ideas of Briand and his associates also came close to something in the nature of a European Federation but involved a process of integration which in the first instance would be economic and as a priority would put in place a framework for amicable relations between France and Germany. Unlike the union of hearts and minds envisaged by Coudenhove-Kalergi, the inspiration for Briand's Europe was internationalist and pragmatic. The Austrian held to his dream, the Frenchman to a method.

To cut a long story short, neither of these approaches to European unity prevented the war of 1939-45. Again, this was a war between nations whose economic and industrial resources were stretched to their limits to propel bigger and more awesome weapons across land, sea and air.

When the war ended it was also back to the drawing board as far as the future peace of the world was concerned. At the global level, the United Nations Organisation was established to step into the role in which the League of Nations had disappointed. On the European scale the notion of a sort of subliminal European consciousness as a political force resurfaced in the Christian Democrat parties which blossomed in the immediate post-war period.

These brought to the fore the new 'Dreamers', in particular Alcide de Gasperi, Robert Schuman and Konrad Adenauer. Although from Italy, France and Germany respectively, these were all of Germanic origin and all practising Catholics. Their shared outlook and common language enabled them to give coherence to what might otherwise have been a rather vague pro-European spirit of the age. Out of this movement came the Hague Congress of 1948 leading to the establishment of the Council of Europe. The momentum was soon lost, however, and it became clear that this was not the foundation for the political integration hoped for by its most ardent supporters. Their energy now went into backing the most influential

'Technician' of the age: Jean Monnet.

Monnet took up the core idea of the pre-war Briand Plan for an institutional link between the key industries of France and Germany. With Konrad Adenauer as Chancellor of West Germany and Robert Schuman as Foreign Minister of France, the essential support was in place for Monnet to make a decisive move. The cornerstone of today's European Union was thus laid on 9 May 1950 at a press conference convened by Schuman. On that fateful occasion he made a declaration, the main points of which were:

1) History teaches that world peace requires a peaceful Europe, which means a united Europe. This requires that France and Germany put aside their age-old mistrust and animosity for each other.
2) France and Germany therefore intend to place all of their coal and steel production under the jurisdiction of a High Authority.
3) Control of raw materials by an independent body will prevent the heavy industry of one nation from ever again building an arsenal to threaten the security of the other.
4) Other European nations are invited to join in this venture, which will be the first stage of an economic community and an eventual European Federation.

This is how the world learned of an idea developed behind closed doors by Monnet and his friends but which was quickly baptised the 'Schuman Plan'.

The hybrid nature of the plan is apparent in the drafting. The first three points plainly come from the pen of a 'Technician':

1) This is the problem
2) This is what we propose to do about it
3) This is the outcome we expect

The fourth, however, has obviously been added to welcome on board the 'Dreamers'. Of course, this was at the time a small price to pay. Without Adenauer and Schuman, the plan would probably never have got off the ground and Europe might have slipped back into rivalry and bitterness as it did after the Great War. On the other hand, the Europe built under these conditions would always be an awkward mixture of styles and ambitions. It is rather as if a factory, in return for support from the local convent, invites the nuns to sit on the board of directors. Nobody then has the bad manners to mention to the sisters that business is business, salvation is salvation and the works is not set up to produce what they pray for. In a nutshell, that has been the mismatch of ambitions at the heart of the European project since Schuman read out his statement. The main concern has been to 'build Europe', but with regard to what sort of Europe and what for, there is a discreet silence over the question.

There was another way in which the Schuman Plan put its own gloss on the reality of the times. Heavy industry in Germany had always been more efficient and more productive than in France. Following the Second World War that competitive edge was lost as Germany output was curtailed by order of the occupying powers, while France pressed ahead with a programme of modernization. France's coalfields could not meet the energy requirements of an expansion on the projected scale but it was anticipated that any shortfall would be made up by deliveries from Germany, where the reduced level of industrial activity would divert coal and coke to export. The logic fell down, however, when a split between the wartime Allies divided Germany and the whole of Europe into East and West. This turned the page on the war against Hitler and opened an era in which the newly created West Germany joined the side of America and the 'Free World' against Russian communism.

This change heralded the end of control over the economic affairs of the West German partner and so raised the spectre of a resurgence of German steel production which would doom France to languish forever in the second rank of Continental industrial economies. To guard against this, the Schuman Plan placed West German resources under an outside authority that would take account of French interests. France would be subject to the same control, as would any other country that chose to join, but the main effect would be to prevent German coal from staying at home to produce a surplus of cheap steel to be dumped on the world market.

What was at stake in the Schuman Plan with regard to its immediate economic consequences is clear. The bare facts of the matter are indisputable. Their interpretation, however, may be stretched to two extremes:

> EITHER the whole purpose was to rescue France's modernization plan from the consequences of an unrestrained revival of the German steel industry. The references to world peace and progress towards a European federation were mere packaging.

> OR the Schuman Plan gave expression to a genuine belief in a federal future for Europe. Economic uncertainty provided an opportunity to move towards a more harmonious way of conducting relations between neighbours as a first step.

7

Similar positions continue to polarize the debate today. Membership of the European Union can either be judged by the tangible benefits it brings at the national level or accepted as a commitment to a greater good. Depending on point of view, the EU is either a natural blend or an unfortunate muddle of two elements: a Europe to work with and a Europe to believe in.

Thus, as Schuman launched the process of European integration, much was implied and much glossed over. The spirit of the age or desperate necessity, a moment of panic or a window of opportunity; for whatever reason, things were moving rapidly leaving the details to be clarified later. In the melting-pot were relations between France and Germany, Europe and the wide world. The language was political, the action was economic. From hope and humanity, pride and ambition a new Europe would somehow be forged but time alone would tell what shape the finished product might take.

## Method and Machinery

On 9 May 1950 the Europe in the making was thus on one sheet of paper. The details were open to discussion but the overriding principle was embodied in the High Authority: control of coal and steel would be taken out of the hands of national governments. A new concept thus entered the public consciousness and a new term came into usage: the new Europe would be **supranational**. Transcending the old order would be rational decisions taken by intelligent people of good will. If Europe was Camelot, the members of the High Authority were the Knights of the Round Table.

Transforming the outline of the Schuman Plan into a functioning organisation would, however, involve less vision and more straight talking. The British government would not accept the High Authority as a starting point and so declined to participate in the discussions which welcomed delegates from France, West Germany, Belgium, Luxembourg, the Netherlands and Italy.

It soon became apparent that not everyone was content to let the fate of his country's heavy industry be decided exclusively by an unaccountable panel of experts, no matter how well meaning. The institutional framework finally agreed therefore had the High Authority flanked by a Council made up of government ministers from the member states, and also an Assembly bringing together members of national parliaments. Supranationality pure and simple was thus diluted by intergovernmentalism on one hand and democracy on the other. This was the novel feature of the European Coal and Steel Community (ECSC) set up between the six founding members in 1951. These same six later went on to sign the Treaty of Rome in 1957, which founded the European Economic Community (EEC).

The institutional structure of this new Community was borrowed directly from the ECSC. The Coal and Steel High Authority was the inspiration for the European Commission, the Assembly became the European Parliament, while the Council of Ministers was unchanged as the intergovernmental arm of the organisation. These remain to this day as the core elements of the European Union.

From the earliest days, this arrangement was compared to a classic federal structure with two houses of parliament providing representation for the citizens on one hand and the specific interests of each member state on the other. To this way of thinking, the EEC foreshadowed something very much along the lines of the American system: the European Parliament was like the House of Representatives, the Council the equivalent of the Senate, while the European Commission had a vocation akin to that of the White House. On this vague similarity the 'Dreamers' pinned all their hopes, but neither faith nor the passage of time could transform the 'Common Market' into a European Federation. The magic did not work, the 'abracadabra moment' never came. The ugly duckling became not a swan but an ugly duck. This is not surprising if we look at the history of the early years of the EEC.

### The Three Frenchmen

Even though it is common for European federalists to claim Jean Monnet as their own, it is by no means certain that this is what the founding father of European unification had in mind. All the same, the defining factor for Monnet was certainly not the limits of the nation state but the scope of the task in hand. If the necessary steps presaged far-reaching change in the long term, it did not matter. History did not have to be a burden dragged around the same hills and fields by one generation and then the next. Monnet no doubt saw that if he broke that vicious circle, the future would be different from the past and did not regard that as a problem. Nevertheless, the vaguely federal characteristics of the result owed more to compromise than to planning.

On the other hand, the EEC obviously had the potential to be progressively moulded into **something like** a federation. The major problem was that the Council of Ministers was most unconvincing as the Senate of the United States of Europe. In any sort of parliamentary system, the matter in hand is debated and then voted upon. However contentious the issue, whatever is at stake, the votes are counted and the motion is passed or it fails. One side wins the argument and the other side loses but both accept the outcome. It was anticipated that, after a running-in period of a few years, business in the EEC would be dealt with in similar manner. If things had gone as expected the Council of Ministers would indeed have begun to resemble an embryonic second chamber but, in the event, evolution in this direction was dramatically nipped in the bud.

The nipping was done by Charles de Gaulle, the haughty and uncompromising President of France. For de Gaulle, supranationalism was an unnatural practice for which he had only contempt. When the EEC was established he had been in the political wilderness but he returned to office in complete triumph shortly afterwards. By 1965 he had consolidated his position and viewed with disgust the prospect of majority voting being introduced the following year according to timetable.

De Gaulle was a former military man and knew that everything was in timing and choice of terrain. In June 1965, the opportunity presented itself for France to take the moral high ground on a detail regarding the implementation of the Common Agricultural Policy. Using this as an excuse, de Gaulle withdrew the French representative from the Council of Ministers in protest and so began the episode of the 'Empty Chair Crisis' which brought the normal operation of the EEC to a standstill.

Within a few weeks the technical point at issue was conceded but de Gaulle continued to leave France's seat empty and insisted that the change to majority decision making should be abandoned. The crisis endured until January 1966 when it was resolved by the 'Luxembourg Compromise'. This stated that, when majority voting was the rule, any country could declare a vital national interest in respect of the matter under discussion. In these circumstances, every effort would then be made to reach unanimous agreement. No provision was made for what would happen if this proved impossible. In effect, the Luxembourg Compromise therefore amounted to a veto.

While this device could be used by any member to bring proceedings to a halt, the conduct of Council business in anything like a parliamentary style was a forlorn hope. Instead of developing as an element of a real European polity, the Council assumed the nature of a rolling conference. Rather than serving as a forum for the legitimate expression of different views, it drifted into a calculating sort of intergovernmentalism for its own sake. This was not quite the diplomacy of Talleyrand or Metternich in the nineteenth century; the threat of the veto was not the same as an army on the frontier. Nevertheless, the notion that the Council was anything like a

European Senate was made to look fanciful in the extreme.

As if this were not enough, the balance of the Community system then became further skewed towards the intergovernmental the following decade under the influence of another French president, Valéry Giscard d'Estaing. In 1974, the leaders of all the member states accepted Giscard's suggestion that they would come together for regular summit meetings, on which occasions they would call themselves the 'European Council'. Like the Luxembourg Compromise, this new practice was not written into any treaty but was accepted as a fact of life. Like the Luxembourg Compromise, it also perverted the normal operation of the institutions and cast further doubt on the nature of the supposed political vocation of the Community.

No parliamentary system is perfect but all operate on the principle of settling differences of opinion by open debate. This familiar routine is the defining feature of a political system belonging to the developed world: win some, lose some, move on. The Luxembourg Compromise put aside this essential characteristic by allowing participants to stop the game if things seemed to be going against them. To this, the establishment of the European Council added the option for awkward questions to be passed up to summit level to be dealt with by the classic methods of statesmanship that were old before the EEC was dreamed of.

From Jean Monnet via Charles de Gaulle to Valéry Giscard d'Estaing, the Community System had thus become a peculiar concoction with little resemblance to a federation in the making. Of course this did not stop the European Economic Community as such from functioning. In fact as the years passed and the membership grew, the EEC with all its operational oddities increasingly became the prime mover of economic and political endeavour across the Continent. We must now look more closely at the means by which this unlikely mixture of institutions has for so long touched the lives of so many.

*Thinking About Europe*

*12*

# 2: WHEELS WITHIN WHEELS

## Law and Order

From the beginning, the intergovernmental dimension of the Community System left Europe at the top of two slippery slopes: on one side a federation, on the other a descent into the conventional form of co-operation between sovereign states. In 1965 the Empty Chair Crisis provided the nudge that settled the matter. Thereafter, an integrated Europe was no longer the adventure of a lifetime but a mere matter of administration. Nevertheless, the very fact that formally constituted institutions were operating day by day to regulate the running of the Economic Community meant that authority was no longer confined to the usual corridors of power. With irresistible Cartesian logic it became apparent that something new had been created; if 'Europe' could decide things, then 'Europe' must exist.

Moreover, these decisions are not mere trifles; what is being made is nothing less than European law. Of course, this is not the stuff of the detective novel or the courtroom drama but almost everything that is manufactured and marketed, grown and consumed, processed and transported is covered at some stage. Generally speaking, it is those activities that are vital to a mature economy in the developed world that come within the purview of European legislation. The weight of goods vehicles, the size of a hen's cage, the ingredients in a bar of chocolate and the technical specifications for thousands of everyday items are covered. The intention is narrowly economic but the effects cannot fail to be in evidence everywhere in a society based on the circulation of goods and money. The result is an agreed set of norms and standards that apply everywhere and affect in one way or another the price and quality of almost every traded commodity. Irrespective of the preferences of the individual consumer, the decision is taken for everyone. Left to himself, the man in the street might prefer cheaper pork regardless of how the pig was fed and housed in its lifetime but he has no choice; the Law is the Law. Thus, the routine working of the European institutions has always been an operation that generates, modifies and maintains a legal framework within which ordinary people lead their lives.

European law pervades the legal system of all member states to ensure conformity with a common purpose. In so doing it provides the medium through which agreements between politicians become everyday reality for the citizen. The consequences are profound but difficult to characterize; the exact nature of a sub-federal European entity combining a transnational jurisdiction with concerted political will defies definition. To describe something that he dimly discerned, passionately believed in but could not explain, Jacques Delors referred to 'an unidentified political object'. More elegant but also perhaps more fanciful is the idea of a 'republic without a state' covering the entire membership. The originators of these formulas are not indulging in invention for its own sake but are attempting to capture the essence of a political space generated almost as a side-effect of economic integration. The decisions taken in Brussels and the things that they affect are part of a world in which ordinary people live and work. Their rights, their obligations no longer exist solely within the domain of the nation-state but overflow its borders to be understood on a larger scale and experienced as the shared outcome of a European legislative process. By accident as much as by design, European law transforms an economic community into a human community.

It is thus easy to appreciate that from the very outset the mundane workings of the Common Market had an effect which seemed to imply a unity above and beyond the functions performed. This was the very essence of everything that came later; without the humdrum routine of the original institutions, there would have been nothing of substance to which to attach new aspirations, new meaning. The European Union of today has a grand title conferred by a solemn treaty but the vast bulk of what it actually does remains the province of the institutions established by the Treaty of Rome. Now as then, they spend most of the millions in the budget, employ most of the thousands of people in the offices, and together make the laws that touch the lives of the citizens. A fair amount has been done over the years to give a greater say to the European Parliament, but the legislative process otherwise remains broadly as it was in the beginning: the Commission **proposes**, the Parliament **discusses**, the Council of Ministers **decides**.

## The European Commission

As the direct descendant of the High Authority, the European Commission preserves the supranational credentials of the original conception. The Commission is the conscience of the European Community; it represents and articulates the greater good and embodies the idea of a level of political and economic awareness above the nation-state. It takes an overview of what is right and proper and ensures that EC policy is coherent and consistent. This is, however, the institution that (at least in certain circles) is synonymous with faceless bureaucracy and centralized power. As the

*14*

nearest thing to a European government, it is the Commission which tends to be cast in the role of the anonymous 'They' who blight the lives of ordinary people with irksome decrees and pointless regulations.

Besides taking the blame for the general way in which things are run, the Commission is also like a government in that commissioners share responsibility and stand or fall collectively, but each takes charge of a particular area of policy. This is covered by an administrative unit known as a Directorate General (DG). These compare to the Ministries of the British political system and feature some familiar names (Transport, Agriculture), but also some specifically European titles (Internal Market, Competition). However, the resemblance is only superficial.

In the first place, the European Commission even today is far from being a federal government, although it is the source of the ideas that go through a sort of parliamentary system to eventually become laws. Where the similarity ends is in the political sterility at the top. Commissioners are nominated by member states but once appointed they are sworn to be independent and to put their energy and experience at the disposal of something greater than party or homeland. They are not in office to take any particular view of society, economics or human nature; they are there to be 'European'.

This is not therefore government as we know it. Government implies politics. Whether in the local town council or the marble halls of a federal superpower, those in office are there because of a political choice by the people whose everyday lives they affect. Without that, there is something missing; a void in which the words 'European Federation' can only ring hollow, however often repeated.

The Commission nevertheless plays a key role as the proposer of laws. To the extent that it sets the machinery in motion, the Commission is indeed the source of the famous Regulations and Directives which often first burst upon the public consciousness as a result of howls of protest in the media. On such occasions the Commission is usually portrayed as less of a government and more of a mad hatter's tea party. There are, however, two points to be born in mind. Firstly, the Commission puts forward its ideas but does not have the final say in whether they are adopted. Secondly, its proposals are not plucked from thin air and issued on a whim.

To the ordinary citizen, the procedures may be obscure and the organization Byzantine but the Commission is by no means isolated from the hurly-burly of politics or the cut and thrust of the world of business. Far from being a closed order, the Commission is open to influence from a wide range of sources through an elaborate system of advisory committees, some made up of experts nominated by member governments, others representing certain industries, specific agricultural products or other economic sectors. At all levels, at every stage, there is specialist advice on whether a proposal is technically feasible, economically viable or politically acceptable. The measures finally taken may come as a surprise to the man in the street but not to the government departments, producers' associations and trade organizations affected. The aim of the Commission is not to foist its plans onto the unwary but to consult widely and take into account all views which have a bearing on the matter under consideration.

In many respects this method makes perfect sense but, at the limit, equates the European common good with an amalgam of vested interests. Perhaps what is best for, say, European sugar producers is also best for the man on the Clapham omnibus, but they have the chance to put their case at an early stage in the proceedings whereas he does not. On the other hand, it is expert advice and inside information that prevent Commission proposals from being mere fanciful notions that have no hope of being followed through.

In regard to the far-reaching decisions that add substantially to European law, the Commission thus acts as a clearing-house for opinions and a facilitator for the legislative process. However, there are circumstances in which the same Commission acts on its own authority and issues rulings which have the force of law with immediate effect. In fact these are usually uncontroversial. Thousands are enacted every year and usually pass unnoticed by the man in the street and unchallenged by the popular press.

Mostly these arise from the powers conferred by the Treaty of Rome. These enable the Commission to regulate the workings of the Common Market by ordering adjustments to the plethora of rules that govern its operation, from competition policy to agricultural price support. For the sake of efficiency, this has to be performed without the need to submit every comma and decimal point to the full treatment. Thus, within an area covering a wide spread of routine business, recurring expenses and common problems the Commission issues the appropriate legislative instruments as required and without further ado. What the Commission does not do is break new ground on its own authority. Great changes in the lives of the citizens and precedents that shape the European Union for the future are not pulled out of the hat but emerge from a process of examination and debate that includes the European Parliament, but in which the key players are the representatives of national governments in the Council of Ministers.

## The Council of Ministers

The European Commission has no exact parallel elsewhere and largely defies description in any terms but its own. Comparisons with the functions of a government or a civil service are illuminating to a point but do not capture the essence of a working institution whose fate is to be supranational in an organizational environment that is skewed the other way. The Commission squares the European circle by undertaking a range of activities by a number of means for a variety of purposes. By comparison, the nature of the Council of Ministers is uncomplicated: it exists to represent the governments of the member states.

Neither is there any mystery about the methods employed, which are as old as time. Ministers with a clear idea of what they want for their respective countries negotiate together and attempt to find a position that all can agree. Objections are expressed, side issues raised and compromises suggested. Every minister from every country seeks allies, persuades or threatens, concedes or resists. It is this presence in the cockpit of the Union that makes nonsense of the fallacy common in Britain that 'we' are being ruled by 'them', by Europe. At least in the sense that **our** government pursues **its** agenda in Brussels, we **are** them, we **are** Europe.

This not quite, however, the classic diplomacy of bygone days. There is room enough for intrigue and manoeuvre but this is not the place where one nation's Master Plan clashes with another's Grand Design. The Council handles what it is given; it is a conduit for ideas developed elsewhere, and what passes through is the stuff of a Europe completely unlike that of Lord Salisbury or Otto von Bismark. Nevertheless, the game today is hardly less serious. With the future of industry and agriculture at stake, with subsidies and contributions to be calculated, Europe remains a patchwork of interests that statesmen trim and adjust as always. There is nothing incongruous in this; the European Union is not founded on obedience and self-sacrifice. Its very structure invites members to define their own objectives *within the system*. The work of the Council consists of reconciling those various points of view to achieve an agreement on the particular subject under discussion.

At this stage, any proposal is out of the hands of the Commission, where impartiality and the greater European good are the golden rules. It is now the centre of attention in an arena where the skills of career politicians are employed in the service of their countries. However, to focus on this competitive aspect is to miss the broader picture. The Council of Ministers is by definition intergovernmental but it is the intergovernmental part of something greater which is, at least notionally, supranational. Member states do not bring their own policies before the Council to see how they can be accommodated; any advantage has to be wrung from the proposals that the Commission submits. The Council takes the decisions, but it does not decide what about. This is the forum in which the nation-states press their views and defend their interests, but without a flow of ideas from the Commission there is nothing to argue over.

It must also be said that intergovernmental is not necessarily synonymous with confrontational. The Council does not always have to be politics red in tooth and claw; in fact a system exists to identify potential clashes and examine the options at a preliminary stage. This support is required not only in the interests of harmony but also because of the volume of work required on each proposal. Because the Council is not in permanent session each member state maintains in Brussels a group of civil servants who perform much of the preparatory work in liaison with their counterparts from the other countries. Together they form a committee universally known by its French acronym: COREPER *(Comité des représentants permanents)*.

When the Commission presents a proposal to the Council it is usually handled in the first instance by a working group set up by COREPER. Meetings include a representative of the Commission and consist of a frank exchange of views without any government committing itself. At the end of its study the working group reports to COREPER either with the basis of an agreement or details of the sticking points. At this stage any technical difficulties have normally been resolved and problems remaining are likely to be more of a political nature. It is now the turn of the Permanent Representatives to negotiate among themselves with a view to reconciling any differences. This is done quietly, between professionals in the manner of ambassadors since time immemorial. Proposals agreed at this level are then passed to the Council of Ministers as business that can effectively be rubber-stamped without further discussion.

A criticism of this procedure is that it leaves the decision to a restricted circle of insiders, an international elite of unelected officials given a free hand by ministers happy to have their load lightened. This is in essence true but COREPER's influence does not have sinister overtones. COREPER has no agenda of its own; it acts as a melting pot for the interests of all the member countries of the EU. Moreover, COREPER may work in the utmost discretion but the agreements it arrives at have to be endorsed by the Council of Ministers, after which they are in the public domain. To the outsider the process may be a mystery but the outcome is plain enough. On the other hand, the lack of transparency throughout leaves the citizen in a poor position to judge the appropriateness of that result against the arguments deployed during the course of its negotiation.

This also applies to the more contentious questions that cannot be disposed of at COREPER level and are left for the Council of Ministers. Here the actors are top politicians from twenty-five democracies, but still the decision is thrashed out in closed session. Not that there is anything clandestine about this. Those present and the subject under discussion are known and the subsequent Directive or Regulation rolls off the printing presses in black and white. Less apparent is who exactly said what to whom.

Despite continuing pressure for increased transparency, Council business remains the most opaque part of the legislative process. From one point of view this is perfectly understandable; back-room diplomacy has always been a job for specialists. However, dealing with things in this manner draws no distinction between the most unscrupulous piece of international machination and the consideration of a proposal from the European Commission submitted in due form. That difference is crucial to the future of the Union. If its destiny is to embody the political rights of its citizens, it surely cannot continue with the practice of doing its most important business 'under the counter'.

## The European Parliament

Openness has never been a difficulty for the European Parliament; on the contrary, it has always been at pains to conduct itself as much as possible like any other parliament in this respect. Its problem has rather been to challenge a system that allowed it little real say in the final decision. The story of Parliament over half a century is thus one of an institution outgrowing a role that was at best consultative and at worst ornamental.

One constant thread running through the history of the European Parliament is the belief that, even though eclipsed by the other institutions for many practical purposes, it should have as far as possible the form and character of a 'real' parliament. This determination was apparent from the outset, when the embryonic Parliament came into being as the Assembly of the Coal and Steel Community in 1952. Consisting of seventy-two delegates from the national parliaments of the six participating countries, this body could claim to have one of the basic attributes of a parliament in that it was representative, if only indirectly. It was these first delegates who assured that the Assembly would also fulfil a second condition fundamental to a parliament: that of independence. There were at first suggestions that the new institution might, share a secretariat with the High Authority and allow into its sessions 'observers' from other international bodies who would have the right to speak but not to vote. These proposals were discounted in favour of the autonomy necessary for the credible exercise of the parliamentary function.

The Assembly also began at an early stage to stretch its terms of reference in accordance with its own conception of its mission. According to the founding treaty, it was required to meet at least once a year to consider the annual report of the High Authority. The Assembly expanded on this minimum in two ways: by holding extra sessions and by establishing committees to monitor developments and offer guidance in the interim. By these means, and with the cooperation of the High Authority, the supervision after the event provided for in the treaty gradually gave way to regular dialogue throughout the year. There were of course aspects of coal and steel management on which the Assembly was not competent, but by being continuously engaged with the High Authority and providing at least a token political presence on technical questions it staked a claim to a recognizably parliamentary domain within the new Community system.

With the coming into force of the Treaty of Rome in 1958, this nucleus grew to an Assembly of 142 members serving all three European Communities. A clear message was sent as early as the first session of this body when members decided to embellish the name and refer to themselves as the 'European Parliamentary Assembly'. In French and Italian this sounded very well but less so in German and Dutch, which resorted to the simpler 'European Parliament' from the outset. Partly to standardize the terminology and partly as a statement of identity this was adopted as the name in all four official languages in 1962.

If the name was relatively easy to acquire, the other attributes of a parliament were more problematical. Most obviously lacking was direct election. This was desirable not merely for its symbolic significance but also because of the practical difficulties of a membership made up of delegates from national parliaments, which meant that its composition varied after every election in each of six countries as members lost their seats at home and were replaced. In conjunction with the level of absenteeism due to the part-time nature of the job, the overall impression was of impermanence and flux.

A decision was finally taken to remedy this situation in 1976, by which time membership had expanded to nine countries, making it difficult to agree on the method of election. The matter was therefore left in abeyance and every member allowed to choose its own arrangements. These generally involved proportional representation, with the exception of Britain which maintained the first-past-the-post system until 1999. Nevertheless, the first elections which took place in 1979 were the expression of a shared heritage of democracy and a commitment to its application on a European scale. On a practical level, the change meant that Members of the European Parliament (MEPs) all took office at the same time and remained for a least one term of five years. Some MEPs also kept their seats at home and exercised a dual mandate but the option of taking on the job full-time was chosen by most of the 410 members. Endowed with greater permanence and a popular mandate, Parliament now possessed the authority to tackle the 'democratic deficit' in the Community System.

Even backed by this new legitimacy, the view of Parliament could simply be disregarded in the Council of Ministers when decisions were taken. It was 1980 before a landmark ruling by the European Court of Justice established the principle that the Council of Ministers must actually wait to **hear** the opinion of Parliament before ignoring it. From there it was six years until the Single European Act (SEA) introduced the 'cooperation procedure' and a further six years until the 'co-decision procedure' in the Treaty of Maastricht of 1992.

The SEA changed a number of articles in the Treaty of Rome which had until then specified that the Council of Ministers should take a decision 'after consulting' Parliament. These now read 'in cooperation with' Parliament. Under this new procedure, both institutions still receive a proposal from the Commission, upon which Parliament issues an opinion. The difference is that now, instead of either heeding or disregarding that opinion, the Council by majority vote adopts a 'common position', which is communicated to Parliament. If Parliament accepts this or does not reply within three months, the Council is free to act in accordance with its stated position. On the other hand, if Parliament replies with a rejection, the Council may still act after giving the matter a second reading but this time voting unanimously. A third option is for Parliament to propose amendments for the Commission to take into account in reformulating its proposal, upon which the Council may then act by majority vote. Nothing prevents a determined and united Council from having its own way but the opinion of Parliament can no longer be dismissed out of hand.

The 'co-decision procedure' introduced by the Treaty of Maastricht takes the involvement of Parliament a stage further. The Commission submits a proposal to the Council and also to Parliament, which issues an opinion. If this endorses the proposal as it stands, or includes amendments that the Council finds acceptable, then the Council may vote the proposed act by a qualified majority. Conversely, if the Council disagrees with the amendments it adopts a common position of which it informs Parliament. Within three months, Parliament may approve or reject this common position; approval means that the act in question becomes effective forthwith, rejection means that it goes no further. The Council cannot overturn this ruling even on the basis of unanimity; the last word goes to Parliament.

Another possibility allows Parliament neither to accept nor reject at this point but instead to propose amendments. In this case, the Council may then adopt the amended text by qualified majority, except for any changes of which the Commission has in the meantime indicated it disapproves, which parts have to be voted unanimously. If the Council does not agree all of Parliament's amendments a Conciliation Committee is convened. This consists of equal numbers of representatives from the Council and Parliament and has six weeks in which to arrive at a text to be voted on by both. If one institution or the other then fails to give this the required majority, or if the Conciliation Committee cannot arrive at a joint text in the first place, the proposal is abandoned.

Also making its first appearance in the SEA was the 'assent procedure'. From 1986 applications from states wishing to join the European Community required both the approval of the Council (acting unanimously) and the assent of Parliament on an absolute majority. Later extended to other international agreements, this effectively gave Parliament a right of veto and thus equal status with the Council in this regard.

Changes to the role of the European Parliament have thus been genuine and far-reaching and have, at every stage, brought it nearer to fulfilling the functions of a 'real' parliament. Still largely absent, however, is a public profile to match.

One of the problems in this regard is the lack of European political parties fighting their cause in every country. In the United States the choice is between Republican and Democrat, whether in Tennessee, Texas or Idaho. There is nothing so simple in Europe, where candidates generally belong to one of the parties familiar to voters at national level. Those parties co-operate as political 'groups' in the European Parliament. Of these, the Socialist group provides a reasonable match for the British Labour Party, the French *Parti Socialiste*, the German *Sozialdemokratische Partei Deutschlands* and other national parties of a similar complexion. On a smaller scale, the same is true for the ecological parties that make up the 'Green' group. Towards the other end of the political spectrum, however, parties have more trouble finding an identifiable banner under which to congregate. Names and composition have varied over the years but there has never been a 'Tory' group or a 'Gaullist' group in the European Parliament. These and similar parties have had to decide if they are more at home in, for example, the European Democratic Group, the Union for Europe or the European People's Party (EPP). This latter is christian democrat in outlook and is a natural point of reference for the *Christlich Demokratische Union* in Germany, but has less in common with the parties of the traditional Right in other countries, which are nevertheless ever tempted to join the ranks for the political weight that this confers. The price is inevitably a lack of ideological coherence.

Not that the electorate seems unduly bothered by what colours the successful candidate will wear in Brussels. In Britain the contest is generally seen as being between Conservative, Labour or Liberal Democrat just as it would be in a domestic election, and the same applies in other countries. A European election is thus treated mainly as a barometer of popularity, thereby reducing it to the status of an opinion poll.

The use of Europe as an annex to the national party-political arena is encouraged by proportional representation (PR), which Britain resisted until 1999. One criticism is that the citizen does not have 'his' or 'her' MP in quite the same way as with the first-past-the-post system because PR cannot work in a single-member constituency. The following example is pure invention and a gross simplification for the purpose of illustration:

> The North Midlands is to elect ten MEPs. Three political parties are contesting the election. Each party presents a list of ten candidates, and voters mark their ballot papers with their choice of party. The turnout is 100 000 and the votes cast are: Conservative: 20 000, Liberal Democrat: 30 000, Labour: 50 000. It is now a matter of reading the successful candidates off each list from the top down: the first five in the case of Labour, three for the Liberal Democrats and two for the Conservatives. Each party thus has a number of MEPs in proportion to its percentage of the vote.

In some ways this is very fair, but the elector is being asked to support a party rather than an individual. Moreover, in this kind of 'fixed list' system it is the party apparatus that chooses the order of the candidates on the list; the nearer to the top, the more likely to be elected. Pride of place therefore goes to close followers of the party line, with the result that a seat as an MEP is more of a career opportunity for the faithful than a chance to speak for the electorate. What should be a solemn duty becomes a secondary function and the office is exercised with more of an eye on national headquarters than an ear to the ground in the constituency. Of course this is a generalization. Certainly there are still MEPs of all parties whose only ambition is to extend a tradition of public service into the expanding field of European Union politics. Obviously there must be more to the European Parliament than a sideshow to the main event in Westminster. All of the foregoing is true but the fact remains that the system itself encourages otherwise, with a consequent loss of credibility and prestige for the European Parliament as an institution and for the MEPs as representatives of the men and women whose votes put them there.

Although proportional representation in Britain tends to make the European Parliament more remote from the man in the street, the effect is mitigated by dividing the country into eleven electoral regions, thus retaining a link of sorts between the seat occupied in Brussels and the inhabitants of a particular part of the home country. This is not the case throughout the European Union, where a national fixed list is commonly used. In this method there are no constituencies and so, from one end of the country to the other, voters are presented with the exactly the same choice on the ballot paper. Each list is compiled by the party concerned and so it is usually the party leaders and their favourites who head the lists and are thus assured of election even though they have no intention whatsoever of sitting in the European Parliament; indeed, some may already occupy seats in the national parliament or other elected positions. Where such behaviour is tolerated or expected, a certain devaluation of the title of MEP is unavoidable when it means little more than one of the lesser feathers in the cap of a party grandee.

The same applies when minority parties that cannot win a single constituency at a general election manage to rally enough support nation-wide to return MEPs to the European Parliament. This tactic has in the past been used with great success by the Hunting and Fishing party in France, or the extreme right-wing National Front in the same country. It could be argued that this is democracy at work and that the campaign slogans of such parties must find a resonance among the ordinary people. So much is undeniable, but the battle for hearts and minds is largely artificial if it revolves around issues which do not figure among the Commission proposals which Parliament is called upon to consider, and to which its working methods are adapted.

Like its counterparts at national level, the European Parliament copes with the large volume of matters upon which it is called to pronounce through a system of specialized committees that examine proposed legislation and present a report. There are standing committees devoted to a range of subjects such as Agriculture, Social Affairs, Regional Policy, the Environment. Places on committees are allocated proportionally according to political group so that the membership is a reflection of the relative strength of the groups in Parliament as a whole. In this way, each committee acts as a microcosm of Parliament itself and has the opportunity to work through any differences of view on a small scale before the matter is debated in plenary session.

A proposal from the Commission thus goes first to the appropriate committee for consideration. For each proposal the committee appoints one of its members as a rapporteur, who researches the matter and presents a draft report to the committee. This is discussed, amended and reconsidered in the meetings that follow until a text can be agreed by a show of hands. The time taken to arrive at this point depends on the complexity and divisiveness of the subject. Eventually a report is produced and a date set for its debate by the full Parliament, on which occasion the *rapporteur* addresses the Chamber as spokesman for the committee.

In outline, this system of passing proposals from specialized committee to full parliament and back again is a familiar one used by national legislatures throughout Europe and beyond. As it stands, the brief description in the foregoing paragraph would put the European Parliament among the world's oldest and finest in respect of working methods. The resemblance is greatly reduced, however, by the inclusion of two more factors: time and space. In the usual scheme of things, the debating chamber of a parliament, its committee rooms and its administrative offices are in close proximity to each other. If not in the same building they will certainly be in the same city for reasons of cost, efficiency and convenience. The European Parliament is unique in that these elements are in three different countries: Belgium, Luxembourg and France. MEPs are therefore often obliged to make a considerable journey to attend to something that should logically entail a walk down the corridor or around the block. Technology may overcome the need to be physically present at the administrative centre in Luxembourg but attending committee meetings and debates in the Chamber on the same day is out of the question. For most of the year Parliament therefore operates on a four week cycle: three weeks in Brussels for committee work and meetings of the political groups, followed by one week in Strasbourg for the plenary sessions.

Even in the age of the lap-top computer, the amount of material transported is considerable. Every month a fleet of heavy goods vehicles leaves Brussels for Strasbourg laden with boxes of files which are returned one week later to be replaced in their cabinets until the next time. Parliament itself has long complained that this situation is ridiculous but has always been the pawn in a game between three countries each looking for the prestige and economic benefits of having the capital of Europe on its soil. The original attraction of Strasbourg was the use of suitable premises, from which Luxembourg unsuccessfully attempted to entice Parliament in 1973 by the construction of a new, purpose-built Chamber. More members and a higher profile have since made playing host to Parliament an even greater prize, creating increased rivalry between France and Belgium, whose governments have spared little expense to provide ever more lavish facilities. Parliament's own choice would be for a permanent home in Brussels, but at French insistence the majority of plenary sessions are still held in Strasbourg. Although the European institutions may be allowed their peculiarities, the peripatetic nature of Parliament cannot fail to add a touch of the circus to its proceedings.

Nor is Parliament's reputation enhanced by its debates in plenary session, which lack the cut and thrust of, for example, the House of Commons. To some extent this is a tribute to the committee system, which defuses many of the potential flash-points. On the other hand, for the public face of a legislative process that affects so many and costs so much, it tends to be a rather dull show that attracts little press attention. Matters are not helped by the obligation for every remark to be translated, making it difficult for members to dispense the sound-bite beloved of journalists. There are few flights of oratory, spontaneity waits for the voice in the headphones, wit and passion disappear into the wiring.

The style of debate also suffers from the need to complete the business in one week per month. For any item on the agenda, a rapporteur will present the findings of the relevant committee. The Commissioner responsible for the proposal then has the right to speak to the motion if he or she so desires. Other members who have put their names down are then called on to speak under strict time limits, with priority being accorded to those recognized as representatives of their political groups. These will already have taken a position and more often than not distributed a statement to the interpreters' booths in advance. As item follows item on the order paper the day's business is disrupted by few hoots, jeers, or newsworthy exchanges.

The businesslike calm of the debates in Strasbourg is, of course, all to the good in as much as it reflects the gravity of the proceedings and the composure of the members, but in fact the restrained atmosphere is aided in no small measure by the high level of absenteeism. Some of the vacant seats belong to members whose time is taken up by commitments at national or local level such as MP, town mayor, or a position in the hierarchy of a political party. Even allowing for these part-timers, the Chamber would doubtless be less empty if the debates were more lively and the participants more open to persuasion. As it is, the script is very much known in advance and the outcome unlikely to dominate the headlines; certainly the government will not be embarrassed, for there is no government. Even for MEPs with an interest in a particular piece of legislation, there is no real incentive to attend as voting does not take place at the end of the debates but at set times, not necessarily on the same day, when a list of motions is read out and a vote taken on each without comment or further explanation. Not that it is unknown in national legislatures for members to miss the debate and then vote on the bill; in a way, Strasbourg merely takes things to their logical conclusion. On the other hand, the European Parliament will hardly gain in public esteem by emulating the very practices that bring 'real' parliaments into disrepute.

There are occasions upon which the plenary session comes alive and may even generate a certain amount of media interest. One such event is the rare procedure of a motion of censure against the Commission with the intention of forcing its resignation. This drastic measure requires a good attendance as it has to obtain a two-thirds majority in the Chamber; the number in favour must also represent more than one half of all the MEPs, absentees included. In practice this is very difficult to achieve. One factor is an obligatory cooling-off period of three days, which may become stretched to a month if no time remains to take the vote in the current session. The delay gives the Commission an opportunity to exercise its influence, and time for MEPs to consider the consequences. To date, this has always been enough to save the Commission from the ignominy of formal defeat, even when in 1999 it was shamed into resigning nonetheless following a scandal. The dilemma for MEPs revolves round the fact that, regardless of the shortcomings of Commissioners as individuals, the Commission as an institution is the natural complement to Parliament; to undermine its authority is to weaken an ally.

The secret is therefore in cooperation. If the Commission puts forward the proposals that Parliament would like to consider, and Parliament is ready to give a sympathetic reading to initiatives that the Commission holds dear, there is the opportunity for mutual understanding. In fact, the Treaty of Maastricht formalized this relationship by a provision allowing Parliament to request the Commission to submit a proposal on a matter identified by a majority of MEPs as requiring attention.

This does not give limitless scope for action, but does at least hold out the promise of some influence over what comes down the legislation conveyor belt. Not that the Commission is exclusively at the service of Parliament. The right of initiative remains with the Commission but it must take into account the general guidelines laid down by the European Council, the priorities set by the revolving Presidency and the results of its own consultation procedure. Even when, despite these constraints, a proposal can be put forward in the form that Parliament would wish, a vote in favour does not automatically see the measure adopted as European Law. The co-decision procedure is like a door with two keys; it only gives Parliament the last word when that word is 'No'. Parliament can block legislation approved by the Council of Ministers but it cannot push through anything rejected by it. There also remains a hard core of subjects for which the consultation procedure applies and the Council can override the wishes of Parliament. Closer links with the Commission may thus allow Parliament a more active role in the legislative process but the system still favours the intergovernmental side of things.

## Regulations and Directives

In brief, any item of legislation begins with a proposal from the Commission, and then takes one of three routes via Parliament and the Council of Ministers according to the subject matter. The procedure involved may be Consultation, Cooperation, or Co-decision. In any case what emerges at the end is a piece of European Law. This loose term covers a range of legal instruments, of which the two most important are Regulations and Directives. These both emerge from the same process described above, but differ in the way they are applied.

In the case of a regulation, it is binding in its entirety and directly applicable in all member states. National parliaments have no say in the matter. The new measure has the force of law throughout the European Union at the same time without further ado.

Regulations always have a general application; that is to say they contain provisions which can be applied as and when required to whomsoever they may concern. For example, a regulation restricting the number of hours that drivers of heavy goods vehicles may spend behind the wheel immediately becomes a legal obligation on all persons employed as such anywhere in the EU. A British lorry driver stopped by British police and found to have exceeded the time limit can be charged to appear in a British court even though the law in question has never been voted in the House of Commons. The very same provisions are likewise enforced by the police and the judiciary in Spain, Italy, Germany and all the countries of the EU. Only exceptionally are local variations allowed on a temporary basis. It is a European law. One size fits all.

A directive is quite a different matter. A directive is addressed to member states and is binding on them with regard to outcome but not method. It defines the overall result that must be achieved but leaves governments the choice of how to go about it. Each country then passes its own law designed to have the required effect. When all is done, the same conditions will apply across the EU but expressed through a variety of legislative instruments according to preferred national practice. Failure to comply is thus a breach of French law in France, or German law in Germany but will involve contravention of the same general principle which is upheld throughout.

A directive therefore sets out what must happen but does not say how, leaving national governments to fill the gap as they see fit. This is therefore rather at odds with the myth widespread in Britain which has European law being handed down from a soulless bureaucracy in Brussels. This is far from the truth. With regard to European Law in any form, British MEPs examine the proposal in the European Parliament, British diplomats exert their influence in COREPER and members of the British government cast their votes in the Council of Ministers. Furthermore, in the case of a Directive, Her Majesty's Government then drafts a bill of its own devising for presentation to a House of Commons where it has a majority. In the normal course of events, the bill is then debated before receiving the Royal Assent. Far from being graven in stone and imposed from on high, a directive therefore contains a good deal of input from nearer to home. This is often the cause of misunderstanding and a source of both deliberate and unexpected side effects that only add to the sense of confusion and unease among those ordinary citizens whose lives are affected in large or small ways.

For example customers at supermarkets are now less likely to find used cardboard boxes stacked near the checkouts for their use. This once-common sight has now largely disappeared as a result of a European Directive intended to reduce the amount of cardboard being disposed of in landfill sites.

In Britain, this was translated into national law by the Environment Act 1995, which was prefaced by the time-honoured formula:

> BE IT ENACTED by the Queen's most Excellent Majesty, by and with the advice and consent of the Lords Spiritual and Temporal, and Commons, in this present Parliament assembled, and by the authority of the same...

In other words, this is in every sense an English (or Scottish) law. Buried within its four hundred pages covering subjects from air quality to hedgerows is a short section enabling the Secretary of State to issue regulations on the reuse, recovery and recycling of waste materials. These regulations appeared in March 1997 and set out procedures by which each business affected would be registered, calculate its recycling obligations for the coming years, and discharge that responsibility officially by furnishing proof of compliance to the Environment Agency. A large retailer therefore has to meet a legal requirement expressed as a specific figure for different types of packaging, including the category of 'paper and cardboard'.

The result is no empty boxes at the checkouts because of the way in which 'reuse' was understood. This was defined as serving for more than one trip *for the same purpose for which it was designed.* In other words a box once containing apples would qualify if returned to the market gardener and refilled but not if taken home by a supermarket customer carrying bottles of wine and tins of cat food. As far as the impact on the environment is concerned, there is no damage done as long as the packaging remains in circulation fulfilling some useful purpose. The fact that this is not officially 'reuse' therefore seems to go against common sense. Of course this is not the end of the world, but these examples illustrate how a directive formulated at the European level and implemented by the member states may have effects that are not explicit in the primary purpose of the legislation and are blamed on 'Europe' or 'Brussels' when it makes as much sense to blame 'Westminster' or 'Buckingham Palace'.

It is clear, however, that the European Union assumes a legal authority of its own that inevitably overlaps the traditional attributes of the nation-state. This raises the vexed question of sovereignty.

This emotive word is used more often for making mischief than for accuracy of expression. 'British sovereignty' or 'the sovereignty of Parliament' are trotted out as handy slogans but do not mean the same thing. The former refers to the freedom of the government of Great Britain to deal with other countries as it sees fit. The latter conveys the possibility that the same government will use its majority to treat the British population as it wishes. Membership of the European Union reduces the government's options in both respects but it is perfectly possible to say so without recourse to language which implies that something precious beyond price is being sacrificed.

On the first point, there is nothing particularly new in Britain's conduct on the world stage being restricted by membership of organizations such as the United Nations or NATO. With the passing of the Empire and the advent of the Cold War, there were few decisions of international importance that the British government could take without consulting a network of allies and partners. The shared values upon which this interdependence was supposedly founded eventually gave rise to the idea of the 'international community' that serves as the arbiter of fair play and decency in the post-soviet era. The concept has no formal standing in the same sense as the United Nations but it nevertheless suggests that a state's scope for action is subject to certain unwritten rules interpreted by a consensus of the world's democracies. To accept this and yet imagine that a last-ditch battle to preserve 'British sovereignty' is being fought against Europe is to harbour illusions that belong to an age long gone.

With regard to the right to enact laws binding on the British people, the European Community has undoubtedly encroached upon the domain of the Mother of Parliaments. In assessing the inroads made by Brussels, however, it is important to bear in mind that legislation originating in Europe often suits the purposes of a British government that has taken a leading role in shaping it. For example the closure of small abattoirs, which was actually Ministry of Agriculture policy, was pursued under the cover of the European Meat Directives. Governmental convenience notwithstanding, the fact remains that a European directive places the British parliament in the position of a sub-contractor, while a regulation bypasses it completely. Clearly, things are not as once they were.

Power has not, however, been drained away from Westminster by stealth. Like all member states, Britain actually made formal provision to recognize the European Community as an additional source of legislation. For other countries this involved amending a written constitution, whereas in Britain the primacy of European law was written into the European Communities Act 1972. The effect was a dilution of the principle that a parliament cannot bind its successors. Usually a law can be undone by a later law. A general election and a different political balance in the Commons always allowed an incoming government to change or repeal any laws passed by its predecessors. This is no longer possible where European legislation is concerned. A new government may push through its own laws on the National Health Service or education but cannot decide the number of hours a lorry driver may spend at the wheel or which sorts of fortified wine may be called 'sherry'. This is true throughout the Community; the very same subjects are out of bounds to the French *Assemblée Nationale* or the German *Bundestag.* In the case of a European directive, the way in which it is translated into national law may be treated differently by a new government on condition that the original objective is achieved. However, even directives do not always leave a great deal of leeway for interpretation; a lot depends on the degree of complexity in relation to the range of technical resources available across the membership. In any event, the purpose of directives is not to offer a sop to parliamentary pride; their flexibility is a matter of necessity.

One way or another, European practice does therefore cut across the principle that national parliaments decide the laws that apply within the frontiers of the state. If this is what is meant by a loss of sovereignty, then it is perfectly true. The problem is that the words are used not so much to express a matter of fact as to imply that the natural order is being overturned and the birthright of a people squandered. If the question must be considered in such terms, the notion that sovereignty is not lost but pooled has less sinister connotations and at least acknowledges that what is occurring is a multilateral process including other countries. The objection to this conception is that sovereignty is by definition indivisible and cannot be shared.

The state of the debate therefore resembles the situation in the eighteenth century when the science of Chemistry was at the stage where it was thought that combustible materials contained an invisible substance called 'phlogiston'. Attempts to explain what happens when substances burn therefore turned on the question of where the phlogiston had gone, with the result that the actual reactions involved could not be thought about in any useful way. The question of whether sovereignty is being lost or conserved in our relations with the EU is likewise just as sterile. The fact is that laws are made where they are made and have the effects they have. Of course this should be a matter for study and comment. We have a right to know exactly what is happening and why, but the hocus-pocus of a bygone age is unlikely to help.

# 3: FLIES IN THE OINTMENT

Almost anyone would agree that the EU needs to be able to act on its own authority up to a point. On this side of the Channel, however, there are some aspects of national life in which European involvement is not unanimously regarded as a good thing.

## The Common Agricultural Policy (CAP)

When the possibility of establishing a European Economic Community was raised in the late 1950s, the idea was that it would be based on a customs union. Members would abolish tariffs between themselves and put in place a customs barrier around the whole Community. Imports from the outside world would enter on whatever terms Europe fixed but goods manufactured within the barrier would circulate freely in a Common Market. For French industrialists, used to a high degree of protectionism, this was a nightmare scenario. As talks about the project dragged on, concessions were made and guarantees given without producing a package which would win the approval of the French parliament and public. The solution was to attach to the Common Market a scheme that would appeal to a broader constituency: a Common Agricultural Policy (CAP). Here was something that would have the support of rural France and at least give the EEC treaty a chance of ratification.

Food is a basic human need and its cost is an important factor in the wage demands of industrial workers. Also, agriculture is an economic sector just as much as engineering or textiles and so has a place in an Economic Community. Nevertheless, the salient point regarding the CAP is that France would never have accepted the Common Market without it. Germany had factories, France had farms: the EEC was a bargain struck between the two.

Not that a Common Agricultural Policy was an intrinsically bad idea. The production and marketing of food were matters upon which the governments of the six founder members of the Common Market already had their own policies. If the customs union was to be accompanied by any sort of unified control over its economic consequences, the agricultural sector was a reasonable candidate for a place to start. Another consideration, however, was the need to adopt a system that would be acceptable to France. In essence this consisted of an open-ended promise to purchase at a guaranteed price all that the land could produce. The result was a disaster. With improved fertilizers, increased mechanization and new techniques of animal husbandry, farm output everywhere rose rapidly to more than the entire population of the six member countries could possibly eat. The surplus nevertheless had to be bought at Community expense and put into storage in what became known as the 'Butter Mountain', the 'Beef Mountain', the 'Milk Lake', *et cetera*. Huge quantities of these products were then routinely sold at a heavy loss outside the Common Market while shop prices within remained high.

It is this waste and expense to the consumer for which the CAP has been most criticised. There is no argument about the principle of supporting farmers; all member states previously offered assistance in some form or other. The problem for European agriculture is that many staple foods can be produced more cheaply elsewhere. For cereal production, the American plains offer economies of scale that cannot be found in Europe. Likewise the herds of beef cattle on the Argentine pampas or the dairy farms of New Zealand enjoy natural advantages that come with vast open spaces. Items like wheat, meat and butter can therefore usually be obtained on the world market at prices with which home producers cannot compete. Other than seeing farms go bankrupt and agriculture disappear, governments had two options. The British tradition was to allow the law of supply and demand to dictate prices; if this meant farmers making a loss, they received a direct subsidy from the public purse to enable them to stay in business. The cost ultimately fell on the taxpayer but prices across the counter were low. The alternative, favoured by some countries on the Continent, was to keep prices artificially high by imposing a tariff on imports so that, for example, Canadian wheat was just as expensive as home produced. The farmer then needed no subsidy but the additional cost of ingredients to the baker was passed on in the price of a loaf. This latter method is the one upon which the CAP was based.

The key to the system is a 'target price' which is set annually for different foodstuffs. Imports of that commodity are then monitored on a daily basis and have a 'variable levy' imposed, calculated at a rate to prevent them being sold more cheaply after distribution costs have been met. The levy can be imagined as a sort of entrance fee paid at the door. If the target price of a particular foodstuff works out at the equivalent of eighty pence a packet and a cargo arrives at Portsmouth that could be sold to the house-wife in Birmingham for sixty pence a packet, the levy charged on each packet unloaded is twenty pence. Of course, the reality is slightly more complicated and the unit of calculation larger but the principle is the same. To stay with the same example, there will also be an 'intervention price' corresponding to about seventy-five pence per packet. If so much of the item is being produced within the Common Market that competition has driven the price down, national intervention agencies are obliged to buy at this figure any amount offered to them by the producer and store it in the appropriate 'mountain'. In effect this represents a minimum price to the farmer.

In theory this system has certain advantages; the problem is that they are not apparent on a day-to-day basis. For example, it is true that the threat of shortage is removed, but there would have to be a worldwide famine for the benefit to be felt. In the case of a failed harvest in Europe alone, simply removing the levy would bring supplies flooding in. It is also true that the CAP has stabilized prices to the consumer, but only by keeping them permanently high. From another point of view the CAP is a gesture towards the social and cultural significance of working the land, but it is the large-scale producer who gains most and the smallholder and peasant farmer the least. Craft gives way to calculation and tradition is sacrificed to quantity.

In fact, the original focus on quantity disregarded the changing nature of the relationship between society and the soil. As more of the population lives in towns there is a certain nostalgia for rural ways and the timeless rhythm of the countryside but, in reality, the link between the crop in the field and the food on the table is ever more tenuous as society becomes less rural and more prosperous. At the heart of the matter is the fact that food has a low demand elasticity; in other words, people can only eat a certain amount and so as their disposable income rises they do not buy larger quantities. The tendency is rather to buy more expensive food. Firstly, there is a willingness to pay for convenience in the form of ready-made pizzas, hamburgers *et cetera* and all kinds of tinned or frozen prepared meals. The important point here is that the farmer gets no more for the basic ingredients; the extra cost to the consumer is in processing, packaging and distribution. Secondly, when fresh produce is purchased, a greater proportion is made up of imports such as exotic fruits and out of season vegetables. Again, the European farmer gains nothing from a more affluent shopper who prefers green beans flown in from Kenya to an extra helping of home-grown turnip.

Faced with this situation, the rational choice for the producer is to maximize output by whatever means to take advantage of the profit to be made at the intervention price. Farmers therefore adapted to a system that rewarded high output. Of the original six countries of the Common Market, this particularly suited France, which had forty-seven percent of the agricultural land and a range of climatic conditions stretching from the

Mediterranean to the English Channel. Nevertheless, every member had an agricultural sector of some sort that could be expanded using modern methods of production. None of the six could rival France for cereals but, for example, by the late 1960s the Federal Republic of Germany was responsible for three quarters of the butter mountain.

In brief, increased production made the CAP a bottomless pit into which most of the budget of the EEC disappeared. The fundamental problem was that there was really only half a Common Agricultural Policy. All that was in place was system of price support, while nothing was being done to rationalize the structure of the sector. The first attempt at comprehensive reform came in 1968 in the shape of the Mansholt Plan, which proposed a shift away from price support in order to reduce the gap between the cost of food produced in the Common Market and world prices. This required increased productivity through mechanization and larger farms. On its own this would only serve to increase the surplus, and so Mansholt also recommended a reduction in the total area under cultivation by turning land over to other uses; for example forestry or leisure activities. The plan made good economic sense but the Council of Ministers struggled with the political decisions and only gradually adopted some of the ideas in dilute form.

The result was a long process that went some way to addressing the worst excesses of the CAP without ever providing a complete solution. This was not good enough for Margaret Thatcher, who mounted a scathing attack on the way that the CAP was run, culminating in 1984 when she famously demanded 'her' money back and got it in the form of an annual rebate on Britain's contribution to the European budget. In the same year milk quotas were introduced, allocated to each member state and then split down to a figure for each producer. In 1988 maximum quantities were fixed for all items subject to intervention buying. These were known as 'stabilizers', each being a threshold beyond which the intervention price was slashed. The 1992 reforms brought in the practice of 'set-aside' by which farmers were paid not to cultivate a proportion of their land. At the same time there was the start of shift from price support to direct income support. There is therefore a widespread acceptance that change is necessary, but progress is agonizingly slow because of the political implications in the countries that benefit the most. Rather than a root-and-branch reform, there will be continued tinkering as the years go by. The main point is that the important argument has been won. There still remains a good way to go but at least reason seems set to prevail in the long term.

## The Euro

Money makes the world go round, and has done for a long time. Certainly, for any organisation calling itself the European Economic Community, money must play a crucial role. Apart from the obvious advantages to travellers, a single currency simplifies things all round. Where tariffs are calculated, subsidies granted, prices regulated and fines imposed, the figures used must have the same significance in all the countries affected. This is an obvious argument for using the same currency throughout the Community, the solution which was eventually adopted by most members.

Before the advent of the euro, efforts were concentrated on trying to peg the values of the various national currencies so that conversion from one to another would be routine clerical work. A first attempt in 1972 earned the name The Snake in the Tunnel from a graph of its variations within upper and lower dollar values. This failed but a fresh approach was tried from 1978 with the European Monetary System (EMS). This had two elements: the Exchange Rate Mechanism (ERM) and the European Currency Unit (ECU). The ECU was an invented currency made up of a 'basket' of fixed amounts of the currencies of member states. Its first function was to serve as a unit of account for EEC administrative purposes, but it also acted as a reference point to assign values to members' national currencies relative to each other within certain allowed limits.

All of this was easier said than done and members sometimes found it difficult to keep their currencies within the permitted band of fluctuation due to speculative pressure via the money markets or lack of confidence in the way the country was being run. In that case, because it was not compulsory, there was always the option of dropping out of the ERM altogether. A second possibility was to devalue the currency with the approval of the other members. In either case, the decision was primarily a political one.

In 1981 France went to the polls and elected a new President of the Republic, a socialist named François Mitterrand. He immediately dissolved parliament and called a general election, which returned a landslide majority for his party. With his position now unassailable, Mitterrand embarked on a radical left-wing economic programme: nationalisations, cuts to the working week, increases in the minimum wage, *et cetera*. Confidence in the currency, the franc, plummeted with the result that it had to be devalued twice within twelve months. With a further devaluation looming, there was a stark choice to be made. France could either drop out of the ERM or abandon socialist principles and tighten the purse strings. Mitterrand chose the latter course on the advice of his Minister of Finance,

Jacques Delors.

Rather than admit that his policies had brought the country to the brink of ruin, Mitterrand put a more favourable complexion on this U-turn by becoming an ardent convert to the European cause; it was for the sake of unity with her partners that France would now endure any amount of austerity in order to stay in the ERM. Helmut Kohl, the German Chancellor, assisted by revaluing the deutchmark upwards, thus maintaining its value relative to the franc without the French currency being devalued downwards for a third time. This was a welcome helping hand but the message was clear for all to read: Germany was the dominant partner.

This situation left few options open to a statesman with Mitterrand's combination of lofty pride and cold realism. With little left to lose, the logical course of action was to make a virtue of necessity and take the European policy to its limit. As an alternative to being the perpetual underdog to Germany, the establishment of Economic and Monetary Union throughout the EEC would at least allow France to hide her shame and exercise some influence.

Decades apart, the parallel between two crucial steps in European integration is striking. In 1950 the key indicators of a vibrant economy were coal mining and steel production. In these respects Germany was a giant and France a dwarf; the Schuman Plan proposed to pool their resources in the name of Europe. By the 1980s the measure of a nation was the stability of its currency. Germany's was of the first rank while the French franc struggled to hold its own. A single European currency would remove the difference.

Things had moved on in thirty years, however. In 1950 the newly-formed Federal Republic of Germany was anxious to distance itself from the Hitler era and make a fresh start. The Schuman Plan offered an opportunity to join with other nations who were likewise looking to the future. Giving away some of its edge in the heavy industrial sector was a price worth paying. In the early 1980s the same incentive was not there to put the economic health of the country at risk. That was to change but only when the Berlin Wall came down and everything changed.

In the meantime, the groundwork was begun when Jacques Delors became President of the European Commission and set in motion the process which culminated in the Single European Act. To move forward the agenda on Economic and Monetary Union, Delors set up a committee consisting of the governors of the central banks of the member states with himself as chairman. The masterstroke was in the terms of reference which Delors gave the committee. He did not ask the governors if economic and monetary union was possible or desirable or if they would accept it. He asked them what would be the best way to achieve it if ever the decision were taken.

After long discussion and astute handling by Delors the result was a route to EMU that all could agree, including the Governor of the Bank of England. The essential principle was that when a European Central Bank was established it should be independent and not subject to political control. Otherwise the method followed was one of parallel progress on the economic and monetary aspects. This involved setting 'convergence criteria' by which prospective members would be judged to establish if their economies were sufficiently in line to enable them to join the single currency. The end result would be achieved in three stages. The first amounted to little more than an effort to co-ordinate policies among members. In stage two, exchange rates would be fixed once and for all. Stage three would be a European Central Bank and a single currency to replace national ones.

This was all very well and good but the problem was to generate the political will where it mattered to get the process under way. The British, in the person of Margaret Thatcher, were implacably opposed to the scheme. More importantly, there was little or no enthusiasm in Germany.

Things changed unexpectedly with the collapse of the Soviet Union. When the Berlin Wall fell in November 1989 it became clear that Helmut Kohl was inclined to seize the historic opportunity to reunite a Germany that had been split in two for over half a century. Kohl's problem was to convince those most concerned that the new fatherland of his vision would not be Hitler's Germany revived. This was the point at which the support of France was crucial. The same as fifty years previously, Germany's honourable intentions could be demonstrated by impeccable European credentials with a French seal of approval. An understanding was reached: Mitterrand would give his blessing to reunification and Kohl would put his full weight behind EMU. For his part, however, he needed to be able to present this in the context of a substantial political project: a European Union.

On the joint initiative of Kohl and Mitterrand, an intergovernmental conference of all members of the European Community was held in Madrid in 1990 to agree a firm plan of action. At this meeting Margaret Thatcher's intransigence clashed with Franco-German determination to press matters to a conclusion, with the result that Britain was completely sidelined by the extraordinary decision of the other eleven to issue their own text to which a British statement of dissent was annexed. This document then formed the basis of Article 25 of the Treaty of Maastricht signed in February 1992, which established a timetable for stages two and three towards EMU. Britain was excused from going the whole way to a single currency.

The road to EMU was now open but more political decisions were along the way. Firstly, a name had to be found for the single currency itself. ECU went very well in French (the écu was even a real coin from days gone by), but was less sonorous in languages spoken further from the Mediterranean. In December 1996, the name 'euro' was settled on as the least offensive to everyone. Politics also entered into the question of how rigidly the rules of membership would be applied. It was early assumed that Italy and Spain, large countries not usually renowned for fiscal discipline and low inflation, would fail the test of the 'convergence criteria' and be unable to join in the first wave. In 1996, however, both announced that their economies were now well on track for them to be able to comply in time. The suspicion was that the measures taken were temporary and that the effort would not be sustained once membership was assured. Furthermore, even the French were not above indulging in a little creative accounting to meet the required targets. The Chancellor is a powerful figure in Germany but is subject to the same pressures as politicians everywhere. Helmut Kohl remained committed to EMU but could not ignore criticism from the *Bundesbank* or a public opinion fearful that the solid and reliable German mark was being discarded in favour of a currency more suited to the Latin temperament.

Matters came to a head at the European Council in Dublin in December 1996, when Germany pressed for a 'Stability Pact' to be signed by all participants in EMU. Other countries would have readily accepted this as a piece of window-dressing but Kohl argued forcefully for something with real teeth that would enable member states to be fined if they strayed from the strict conditions originally envisaged. A compromise was eventually agreed that would excuse laxity on the part of any member suffering a manifest recession. To please the French it was also renamed the Growth and Stability Pact.

This gesture was enough to unblock the process which culminated in the issue of the coins and notes of the new money in January 2002. These circulated alongside the old, familiar national currencies for a brief transitional period which varied from country to country. And that was that. Anyone who had previously been rich or poor in francs, pesetas or guilders was now just as rich or poor in euros. People who had never had any influence over wages, prices or interest rates were not surprised to find that somebody else still made those decisions for them. Everyone adapted to the new money in their pockets and life went on as before.

The single currency carried, however, a particular symbolism which stemmed from its use in every corner shop and café in the euro zone. Of all non-cultural expressions of identity, money must rank with law as an aspect of everyday life that helps to define a people. From New York to Seattle, across one state and the next, the same currency is used all along the route. A dollar to one American is a dollar to another. Likewise from Brisbane to Melbourne, the right to spend the same coins and banknotes in Queensland as in New South Wales is part and parcel of an awareness of being Australian. The move to a single European currency therefore gave some substance to the idea that the economic integration which had been in progress for forty years could be the vehicle for a deeper political union.

Politics is in fact an inseparable part of the euro question. Of course it is nominally about money, but in most of Europe that no longer matters. The economic pros and cons of a single currency are the same as they always were. That argument has never been won or lost but was swept aside by a effort of political will from France and Germany. This is not to imply that political motivation is in some way less valid than economic reasoning as a basis for action. Politics is driven by circumstances, and circumstances change, but neither are economic conditions fixed for all time. Within a few years of making such an issue of it, even Germany was chafing against the constraints of the Growth and Stability Pact. To take another example, Britain declined to join the Coal and Steel Community in 1950 because of the huge importance of coal mining to the national economy. Today that seems like a different world, and all of the five pound notes in the Bank of England did not stop the march of time.

All we can honestly say about the future is that we do not know what is coming next. Nor does this only apply to the man in the street. There is more than a grain of truth in the joke that an economist is someone with the expert knowledge to explain why he was wrong last time. The technical arguments surrounding the euro are complex but the choice boils down to which of two attitudes we are most comfortable with. On one hand we can think that, whatever the future may bring, the continued existence of the pound sterling will give Britain the best chance of reacting to changing times in her own way and on her own terms. On the other hand we can take the view that perhaps there are challenges ahead that would be better faced alongside the countries in the euro zone. Looked at in this way, the euro debate takes on a new perspective as only one element of the broader question of where we think the world is going and what we expect to be able to do about it.

**Defence Policy**

From the very outset, economic integration was presented as something which would give Europe a purpose and meaning in the wider scheme of things. In May 1950, the project to form a Coal and Steel Community stressed the contribution that a well-organised and thriving Europe could make to civilisation and world peace.

This was a fine ambition but in practical terms it involved occupying a political space somewhere on an international stage that was dominated by two superpowers and their military alliances. Across the entire globe, East and West were synonymous with Soviet Russia, at the head of the Warsaw Pact, and the USA, leading the North Atlantic Treaty Organisation (NATO). In an age when political clout was a function of military strength, Europe had to shape up or keep quiet. Attempts to follow the Coal and Steel Community with a European Defence Community (EDC) complete with a European Army dragged on until 1954, when the project was rejected by the French parliament. An alternative plan resulted in the creation of the Western European Union (WEU), a mutual assistance pact with a rudimentary organisational structure but little else.

The WEU held meetings and went through the motions of keeping itself occupied but soon faded into the background while the real credibility of European defence was supplied by the United States through NATO. Because much of the money and military muscle of this organisation was American, the USA enjoyed a pre-eminence in the alliance, a situation which the other members readily accepted.

This changed when Charles de Gaulle became President of France in 1958. De Gaulle was an accomplished statesman with an unshakable belief in the destiny of his country among the first rank of global players. As the high priest of the greatness of France he regarded any sort of outside inter-ference in his conduct of the nation's affairs almost as blasphemy. We have already seen how, in 1965, this caused him to attack the supranational principle of the EEC and skew the institutional balance in favour of the member states. The following year he was ready to teach the same lesson to NATO.

The corner-stone of NATO was the integrated military command that took charge of the various national forces assigned to combined military operations. This meant training exercises and manoeuvres in peacetime and, in the event of a war, complete control of the troops sent by member states to take part in the battle for western Europe. In either case, the totality of air, land and sea forces came under the authority of the Supreme

Commander at allied headquarters, who was always an American. In 1966 de Gaulle withdrew French forces from this key part of the Atlantic Alliance and required the removal of all NATO personnel from French soil, including the purpose-built headquarters in Paris.

This did not involve revoking the North Atlantic Treaty itself and did not affect French participation in the other councils and committees of the organization. The crux of the matter was that France remained committed to the letter of the treaty but declined to be bound in advance with regard to what contribution she might make to the alliance in the event of a war. Taken at face value, this implied that the use of French territory by allies arriving to defend western Europe would not be rehearsed, could not be taken for granted, and would be decided on only if the situation arose. In reality, there was no real doubt about which side France would be on if World War Three started. What was difficult to swallow was the idea that when the alarm sounded French forces would be transferred to the control of an American. Nobody denied that France could hardly fail to become embroiled in the conflict but it was to be understood that the President of the Republic would make the final decision on the day and, in the (likely) event of French troops being deployed, they would be fighting for France, under a French general and flying the French flag.

This position contrasted with that of France's European allies, who actually drew comfort from the knowledge that their forces were integrated into a system underpinned by the military might of the United States. In proclaiming loud and clear that such dependency was beneath the dignity of France, de Gaulle was taking a stance from which his successors later found it difficult to retreat. Their problem was that, as European integration increasingly implied political co-operation, a policy of splendid isolation left France with nothing to say on an important aspect of external relations.

The only purely European organisation with competence in military matters was the Western European Union, which by the 1970s had been all but forgotten. From the French point of view, however, it had the great advantage that the USA was not a member. For this very reason, it took many years of manoeuvre and persuasion before France's partners were convinced that the WEU could play a useful role without damaging NATO. On the understanding that this was not the intention, France's fellow members allowed themselves to be persuaded and the WEU was officially reactivated in 1984. As new countries joined, the WEU achieved a membership which was practically the same as that of the European Economic Community, making the case for some sort of link between the two.

Last to accept the idea was Great Britain. By 1991, the other members, although not matching France's enthusiasm for a European defence identity based on the WEU, at least saw no harm in it. For their part, the British stood firm until the negotiation of the Treaty of Maastricht. Of the twelve leaders around the table, eleven were ready to commit to Economic and Monetary Union and to include a section on social policy. John Major, the British Prime Minister could agree to neither, and was faced with the difficult task of arranging for Britain to be exempted from both. This was achieved by giving ground on another point and accepting that the WEU would be brought within the forthcoming treaty.

Thanks to this piece of bargaining, Maastricht announced the advent of a Common Foreign and Security Policy (CFSP) based on a spirit of loyalty and mutual solidarity under the general guidance of the European Council. The treaty guardedly refers to the 'eventual' framing of a common defence policy, which might 'in time' lead to a common defence as a military reality. Without any explanation, the WEU is introduced in the text as 'an integral part of the development of the Union'. Among the British public hardly an eyebrow was raised at the sudden appearance in an important European treaty of an obscure organization from the 1950s as if this were the most natural thing in the world. While much attention was given to the British opt-outs from monetary union and the social chapter, the peculiar sleight-of-hand by which the new European Union obtained a military wing went largely unnoticed.

For the moment, however, nothing existed beyond this sweeping statement of principle. To put some flesh on the bones was quite another matter. During the intergovernmental conference which ran throughout 1996, it became clear that the French preference for WEU members' obligations to be transcribed word-for-word into the new treaty then being prepared would not be accepted. Consequently, the 1997 Treaty of Amsterdam provided only for the EU to 'avail itself of the WEU' in matters having defence implications and left it to the Council to make arrangements for this as and when required.

The Treaty of Nice signed in 2001 had even less to say on the subject. In fact, the text only mentions the WEU to allow for the possibility of bilateral co-operation between any of its members provided that this is not to the detriment of European Union policy. Gone is the declaration that the WEU is 'an integral part' of the Union or any idea that the Council might 'avail itself' of its services. The WEU thus all but disappeared from the defining pages of Europe upon which it had burst so abruptly. In the space of nine years and three solemn treaties it had gone from resurrection to redundancy while on this side of the Channel its arrival by the back door and its later unceremonious relegation to a footnote were greeted with equal indifference.

Of course the general lack of interest was partly because reviving the WEU and bringing it within the existing structures corresponded to a particularly French vision of Europe. This is not to say that the story is simply one of France attempting to open up a strategic and political space which she could claim as her own in the style handed down from Charles de Gaulle. Certainly the French stance had always been squarely in that tradition but was also based on some very real questions about what Europe could or ought to mean. Even as the Treaty of Maastricht was signed, however, the whole context in which those questions were looking for answers was beginning to change beyond recognition.

In November 1989, just over two years before the Treaty of Maastricht, the fall of the Berlin Wall heralded an astonishing transformation of the European political landscape including the reunification of Germany and the complete disintegration of the communist bloc in the east. Even as the WEU was being written into the treaty, without the glowering menace of an enemy on the other side of the frontier, even NATO seemed to have outlived its purpose. After decades of soul-searching, the European Union had treated itself to the sort of military wing that was as outdated as the maps were soon to be.

With the end of the communist bloc in eastern Europe, the western allies were suddenly left with no ready response to a volatile situation which they had never foreseen. Nor was trouble confined to faraway corners of the former Soviet Union but erupted in Yugoslavia, a popular destination for tourists from all over the European Union. Where once families had relaxed on the beaches or enjoyed the charm of the old towns there now unfolded scenes of unspeakable horror as the country descended into a brutal civil war. While in Brussels committees met and reports circulated, in Bosnia people were herded together and killed without pity in the name of 'ethnic cleansing'. While western democracy sat muscle-bound by procedure and technology, a few miles away men, women and children were being slaughtered in thousands with medieval simplicity.

In the name of everything civilized, the situation cried out for action but the existing structures proved ill adapted to decisive intervention at short notice. As an international response gradually took shape, European countries provided troops for peacekeeping under the auspices of the United Nations, and the EU acting under its own colours even took over the administration of the divided town of Mostar. Task forces drawn from various sources operated here and there under the vague co-ordination of an international 'contact group' but this motley military presence was not enough to prevent continuing lawlessness and bloodshed. Finally the political will was conjured up to deploy the overwhelming strength of NATO and peace of a sort was eventually restored to the area. Then it only remained to gather the accounts of the atrocities and exhume the grisly contents of the mass graves. But if Bosnia and Kosovo became bywords for inhumanity, they also symbolized the inertia of the western world in general and the European Union in particular in the face of an untidy but unoriginal crisis of relatively manageable proportions.

In the aftermath of the conflict, however, there was the opportunity for old ideas to be revised in the light of events. British and French attitudes towards NATO had always differed over the preponderant weight of American policy in the organization. Britain saw this as perfectly normal, France as a humiliation. Both now agreed that it could sometimes be inconvenient. In the light of experience, there now seemed to be a case for having a less cumbersome response than NATO available for troubles on a smaller scale. In December 1998, the leaders of both countries met in the French town of Saint-Malo and announced that they would co-operate closely to form the nucleus of an operational capability under the aegis of the EU.

Building on this initiative, plans took shape and, in November 2000, a conference of EU defence ministers announced that by 2003 the Union should be able to deploy at short notice up to 60 000 troops and sustain them in the field for at least a year. This capacity to put forces on the ground was not intended to rival NATO but to allow Europe to react rapidly to local crises without necessarily having the full Atlantic Alliance on board. Should the need arise, a similar scenario to the conflict in Bosnia could be dealt with as a local matter by the European Union.

It is, however, a common failing of military planning that it prepares for the last campaign rather the next. In September 2001 the United States was the victim of a terrorist attack of dreadful proportions. Following those events, American power was projected across the world to seek out the perpetrators in Afghanistan in a demonstration of political will and global reach that the European Union could not hope to match. When the 'war on terrorism' then shifted to Iraq, there was no united response from the European Union. Worse, the two countries with the most influence pulled in completely opposite directions; France being implacably opposed to any military intervention, while Britain actively supported US action with troops on the ground.

The episode served to highlight an underlying problem which could have been brought out by any international crisis. This had been raised periodically over the years in the form of a question: When the President of the United States wants to speak to Europe, who should he call? The point is that there is no one person at the helm with the same sort of authority as the occupant of the White House. When the European Union was established it continued the practice of the EEC, which was to have a rotating presidency occupied for six months at a time by one of the member states. This no longer seemed adequate, given the inclusion of a chapter on Foreign Policy and Security. Even though this was as yet devoid of substance, its very existence on the pages of a formal treaty prompted calls for the creation of a permanent post to front the new initiative.

Another treaty, a change of government in Britain and a war in the Balkans were to intervene before the position was filled in 1999. The object was to install a figure of suitable standing who would be actively involved in policy formulation, treat with ministers on equal terms and speak to the world for the European Union as a single entity. Javier Solana, the first occupant of the position, was a respected politician who had served as Secretary General of NATO and his nomination therefore signalled that this was more than a token appointment. Henceforth, Europe would actively engage with friend and foe, partner and rival on a full-time basis.

In less turbulent times this might have been enough, but the terrorist attacks of 11 September 2001 changed the world in a way which was beyond the scope of this small departure from the tradition of a Europe in which everyone takes a turn and everyone has a say.

Leaving aside the rights and wrongs of the invasions of Afghanistan and Iraq, these were clear demonstrations that the United States could find within its government and its people the will to project overwhelming strength around the globe. The European Union does not have that sort of power to unleash, but neither does it have the political cohesion to act even if it had the means. The question then comes back to the old one about the chicken and the egg: which comes first? In the 1950s, the supporters of the ill-fated European Defence Community saw very clearly that the creation of a European Army must have political integration as a direct consequence. When the EDC failed, the project for a European Political Community was also scrapped because its *raison d'être* had gone. Then, as now, the link between the two was obvious: there has to be some sort of legitimacy attached to the decision which sends men and women away from home to fight and perhaps to die. Clearly, the capability to use military force in pursuit of an interest requires a political identity to define that interest and take ownership of it. But is the converse true? Does a political community need an army in order to sustain a credible agenda of its own in international affairs?

We are not talking here about a return to the gun-boat diplomacy of the Victorian age, but the practical implications of an ambition which was inherent in the process of European integration from the very start. In May 1950 when Robert Schuman made the announcement which formed the basis of the Coal and Steel Community, he emphasised the beneficial role that a united Europe could play at a crucial time in world history. But if Europe was to be an actor on the international stage, the subject of defence arose as a matter of course. To be prepared to adopt a position on questions of global importance and yet remain mute and impotent with regard to the security of Europe's own borders was a half-hearted sort of participation in the great game of power politics which shaped the second half of the twentieth century. With the failure of the European Defence Community, military matters were left exclusively to NATO, while the EEC picked up the economic side of things.

This was not a problem as long as the EEC stuck to its core activities of tariffs and trade. As it began again to lean towards a more political reading of its role, however, this division of labour undermined the cohesion of purpose that would give substance to the idea of a shared destiny. If the subject of defence was taboo, there was a hole at the heart of Europe that commerce and agriculture could not fill.

The argument about a European military capability is thus split three ways. Firstly, the eurosceptic view is that any ambitions extending beyond the Common Market into the political sphere are unwelcome in any event. Secondly, the Atlanticist perspective accepts that the EU should have a political dimension but sees no reason why this should not play second fiddle to the United States. The third school of thought still has the EU as a natural ally to the US but with the ability to rely on its own mettle if it feels compelled to act when and where America does not want to get involved.

Towards the end of 2004, Ukraine teetered on the brink of civil war amongst bitter accusations of dirty tricks in the presidential election. Observers from the European Union reported that there had indeed been enough irregularities to render the result invalid. Happily, political pressure was effective in bringing about a new election and in getting the result accepted. To some extent the outcome was a convincing demonstration of the influence that the EU can wield without the threat of force. But what would have happened if things had turned out differently? Because it worked, the European response comes under the heading of firm diplomacy. If it had failed it would have been nothing but ineffectual bleating. Supposing the Kremlin had sent in the Russian Army to support its favoured candidate, what could the EU have done to prevent Ukraine becoming another Chechnya?

The episode neatly illustrates the three possible attitudes outlined above. In such circumstances the EU should either:

1) Not get involved in the first place
2) Take a stance and count on American support
3) Be ready to back up words with action.

It is simply a question of matching our idea of what sort of European Union we want with the means to do the job as we see it.

# 4: THE GHOST IN THE MACHINE

## Ever Closer Union

The Europe that we have today is built on the Community System, of which the first example was the Coal and Steel Community. The less well-known European Atomic Energy Community followed the same pattern of sectoral integration, but the first major step towards the European Union in its present form was the more general European Economic Community, also known as the Common Market.

This was, and still remains, basically a customs union. This means that manufactures or agricultural produce coming from, for example, the United States are charged the same duties whether landed at a French port or an Italian one or flown into Germany. In effect, the destination becomes 'Europe' pure and simple as far as the costs and formalities involved in bringing the goods to market are concerned. It is not the British government that imposes the tariff on cargoes arriving at Southampton, nor the Dutch government for shipments unloaded at Rotterdam; the rate is fixed in Brussels and the money raised belongs to the European Union. As in any kind of union, the rule is 'one for all and all for one'. The whole question of where Europe is going turns on how far this principle should be extended beyond the purely economic sphere.

To everyone involved, the Common Market was worth doing in any case, but some were always ready to read more into it. It is rather like Christmas. Everyone enjoys the food, the gifts and the general mood of celebration. Some, however, emphasize the 'real' meaning of Christmas and are at pains to ensure that the more spiritual aspects are given due attention along with the commercial side of the festivities. In the same way, the economic aspects of the Common Market were accompanied by a sense that there must be more to it than that. The result was the European Union. Again, like Christmas, there was a long period of anticipation while nothing seemed to happen, then everything came together in a final flurry of activity.

The story starts with a few words at the beginning of the Treaty of Rome. By 1957 when the treaty was drafted, the times were less conducive to grandiose declarations than in 1950. It was still hoped that a better Europe could be founded on the new project to which the six members of the Coal and Steel Community would now subscribe, but the European Federation promised in the Schuman Plan now seemed too ambitious. On the other hand, something along the same lines needed to be included rather than seem to abandon completely the spirit of the text which founded the Community System. Thus, instead of an eventual federation with no idea of how this would be achieved, the new treaty anticipated an 'ever-closer union of the European peoples' with no mention of what this might mean.

This formula is remarkable in expressing a definite goal in conjunction with the idea that it will never quite be achieved. As a nod to the 'Dreamers', it was a fair enough tribute to the idea that something more noble was to be read between the lines. All the same, the Treaty of Rome gave the impression that a federation was now the Europe which dared not speak its name, as page after page set out in minute detail a timetable for the establishment of the customs union and the Common Agricultural Policy, with only the vague phraseology of the preamble recalling any deeper significance. It is, however, a typically British mistake to regard such passages as merely decorative because they appear to mean nothing. Words can serve as a peg for ideas or a handle on events and time alone can tell what use will be made of them.

By 1972 the practical objectives the Treaty of Rome had been largely achieved and the EEC was ready to expand to include three new members: Britain, Denmark and Ireland. A stage had clearly been reached when a decision might be taken regarding what to do next. Nor was this a question for ardent federalists alone; there was a more widespread feeling that the Community had the potential for further development of some sort. The possibilities were therefore explored in October 1972 at a summit meeting in Paris bringing together the leaders of the six member states plus those preparing to join. It was thought that economic and monetary affairs, the environment, social policy and external relations might be tackled within a framework attached in some way to the existing EEC. Unable to decide what precise form this should take, the summit adopted a German proposal nevertheless to present the general idea under a suitably imposing label. The final statement consequently affirmed the intention of the member states to 'transform the whole complex of their relations into a European Union' before the end of the decade.

The deadline was to prove impossible to meet but the bare bones of what a European Union might possibly be were contained in that statement. In essence it meant that members acknowledged a solidarity not explicit in the treaties already signed but which could find expression in a variety of ways. Some of the activities that they undertook might not be Community business strictly speaking but would be dealt with by recognizing new areas of cooperation within or without the existing rules as required. The bedrock of the system was the EEC; the European Union would comprise the EEC plus anything else that its members did together.

In December 1974 the European Council asked one of their own, the Belgian prime minister, Leo Tindemans, to produce a report that would be a reasonable synthesis of the views collected. This was no easy task and left Tindemans on the horns of a dilemma. If his report were too precise, there was bound to be controversy between governments over this or that detail; if it were too vague, it would not contain anything to form the basis of a real plan of action. Tindemans was a Christian Democrat and therefore a federalist by inclination but he denied his own instincts and presented a report setting out a series of practical measures that could be implemented without a new treaty. Quite deliberately he did not put forward anything like a draft constitution for a new Europe but aimed to reinforce the existing institutions by a process of gradual mutation that would give them more authority, more legitimacy and more effectiveness. However, by trying to please everyone Tindemans pleased nobody and no action was taken on his report, which nevertheless served to establish the principle that a European Union might evolve from the structural elements already in place and a change in working practices.

As time went by, the institutions of the European Community were in any case creaking under the strain of a higher workload and an increased membership. In December 1978 the task of proposing improvements was entrusted to a special committee known as the 'Three Wise Men'. Their report called for the conduct of business to be streamlined by means of increased majority voting, greater accountability and closer relations between the institutions. Part of their brief had also been to assess progress towards a European Union. Privately they felt that much talk and no action had reduced this term to empty jargon and that, left to themselves, they would prefer not to use it. Nevertheless, they had their instructions and so inserted a bland statement to the effect that anything to strengthen the internal cohesion of the Community and facilitate its relations with the rest of the world represented movement towards the desired European Union. For the sake of something to say, the idea was thus perpetuated that the EEC could be upgraded to a European Union through a rolling programme of improvements.

Although no immediate action was taken, the expression 'European Union' was henceforth an accepted part of the vocabulary of political discourse to denote something manifestly desirable, lacking in detail for the moment, but within reach for a small effort. What this might entail in practice emerged as, with repetition, certain ideas became received wisdom. By the time the subject was considered by the European Council meeting in Stuttgart in June 1983 the broad outline of what was involved had been traced and retraced in document after document. The Solemn Declaration on European Union signed by the leaders confirmed its omnibus nature:

> European Union is being achieved by deepening and broadening the scope of European activities so that they coherently cover, abeit on a variety of legal bases, a growing proportion of Member States' mutual relations and of their external relations.

There was a broad consensus that the range of improvements generally envisaged implied a political framework of some sort. In 1985 the 'Dooge Report' concluded that this presupposed a population of European citizens on whose behalf decisions would be taken. Those decisions might be on the basis of the Community treaties or through intergovernmental channels but in either case they should come under the same umbrella.

In more than ten years of talking since the Tindemans Report, a reasonably clear idea had thus emerged of what a European Union might be. Basically, it was thought that the EEC could serve the purpose if its institutions were strengthened and if some means could be devised by which the Union could conduct its own foreign policy. So far, so good, but this was all still conjecture nearly thirty years after the founding treaty had been signed in Rome. As then, it was again commercial matters which provided the impetus. The result was the Single European Act (SEA).

The story of the Single European Act begins in 1985 with the appointment of Jacques Delors as President of the European Commission. A French socialist and former Minister of Finance, Delors was to prove a dynamic and determined President, earning himself an unflattering reputation for stubbornness and arrogance in the process, especially among British political circles. In fact Delors was a more complex character than this image would suggest and, above all, shared with Jean Monnet the belief that ideas and action must go together. Monnet relied on charm and persuasion whereas Delors employed other methods but the technique was essentially the same: fix a realistic objective, prepare the ground, move at the right moment.

The new president arrived in office to find already in circulation a paper on the advantages of completing the internal market by removing the remaining obstacles to free trade between members of the customs union. After testing opinion in European capitals, Delors concluded that this was a worthwhile and feasible project and so he ordered a report from the Commissioner concerned, the English peer Lord Cockfield. The result was a document setting out in meticulous detail nearly three hundred separate measures that would be required and a precise timetable leading to a finishing date in 1992.

The SEA was signed in 1986 and work began to deal with the items on Cockfield's list. For once, major changes took place in the full glare of publicity. A huge public information effort was undertaken and few were left unaware that 1992 was to be a landmark in the history of Europe. With a broad consensus on the overall objective, the next six years saw the difficulties addressed one by one and overcome. Technical barriers to trade were dealt with by mutual recognition subject only to the definition of certain fundamental criteria at Community level. For instance, European norms might ensure that lawnmowers cut the grass and were safe to use. Any member state could still enact legislation requiring that its own producers fit a horn, headlights and speedometer, but would not be able to block the import of machines from outside without these accessories. This example is, of course, invented but illustrates the general principle involved for manufactures. Food presented similar problems but with an additional cultural dimension. For a lawnmower company to come under pressure from cheap imports is business; for traditional cheese making to be threatened in the same way is something akin to an invasion or an epidemic. To take an actual example, German beer is brewed to a law of 1516 stating that only wholesome, natural ingredients may be used. The Single Market gave German consumers the opportunity to drink imported beer produced to a lower standard. Nobody is obliged to buy the product but stockists have a right to display it for sale in Germany just as in the country of origin.

Such visible indications of the change taking place attracted much of the attention as the Cockfield proposals were worked through and the target date of 1992 approached, but they in fact were only the tip of the iceberg. Less obvious but equally important was the opening to competition of the service sector including banking, insurance, entertainment, tourism and transport. Also to be tackled were considerations such as the harmonization of taxation, public procurement policies and the free movement of capital. Border controls, administrative procedures and documentation all needed to be brought as much as possible into line. This mammoth task was completed on time with a few exceptions and so the promise of a true Common Market was realized thirty-four years after the Treaty of Rome by the determination of a French socialist and the attention to detail of an English lord. On its own this was already a real achievement, but the Single European Act which made it possible was also a landmark in another way.

In Britain, the term 'Single European Act' was generally taken to imply that the purpose was to produce a 'single Europe'. In fact it meant that it was a single document dealing with more than one European subject. So, while the headline purpose of the SEA was to enable the Cockfield Report to be implemented, the opportunity was also taken to include a number of things that had been in the air for a while but had not yet been brought into a formal treaty. It so happened that these bits and pieces reflected ideas accumulated over the years about what shape a European Union might take:

1) The preamble to the SEA confirmed that the signatory states were resolved to transform relations between themselves into a European Union, which would operate under Community rules where applicable but on the basis of intergovernmental co-operation where foreign policy was concerned.

2) The Council of Ministers would meet at least four times a year at the level of Foreign Minister with a view to formulating and implementing a European foreign policy. The same ministers would also be permitted to discuss such matters at ordinary meetings of the Council. At international conferences ministers would be expected as far as possible to adopt positions agreed with their European colleagues.

3) Nearer to home, the SEA included basic provisions for the implementation of a European social policy.

4) With regard to institutions, the new 'co-operation procedure' gave, on certain subjects, a greater say to the European Parliament than the existing requirement that it be 'consulted' before a decision by the Council of Ministers.

5) At the top of the institutional tree, the European Council was for the first time defined in a formal treaty. According to the SEA it was to bring together, at least twice a year, the Heads of State or of Government assisted by their Ministers for Foreign Affairs and with the participation of the President of the European Commission.

6) For the future, the SEA also contained a vague commitment to progress towards economic and monetary union.

None of these extra provisions were necessary to the establishment of the Single Market, and were certainly regarded in some circles as mere window-dressing. Nevertheless, they outlined the kind of European Union that had been talked about for years: a more democratic EEC with, on one hand, something to say about the lives of the men and women who kept its economy turning and, on the other, the means to present a coherent identity to the wider world. From champion of the workers to player on the international stage, there was between the lines of the SEA a clear sense of a political conception of Europe.

Of course, there were those, like many in the British Conservative Party, who felt that this was the sort of nonsense to which one had to pay lip-service in order to obtain the benefits for business of the Single Market. When it later transpired that the SEA was the thin end of the wedge, it was often said that Margaret Thatcher, the then Prime Minister, should have looked more carefully at the small print before she signed it. In fact the SEA was signed by Lynda Chalker on behalf of Her Majesty the Queen, but that is not important. The point is that the sketchy European Union that could be glimpsed here and there in the text might easily have been left without substance; an occasional token gesture could have spun out any progress over decades. On past performance, the expectation of the British government that this could be arranged was well justified.

In the event, however, circumstances conspired to bring to the fore the main purpose of European integration from the start: to provide the conditions in which France could get along with Germany. As we saw earlier, the moment came when the former wanted a single currency and the latter wanted reunification. A European Union would serve as a suitable framework for both.

Besides provisions for introducing and operating the euro, the Treaty of Maastricht thus also included the ingredients of a political union which had been in the air from the Tindemans Report onwards. The list was by now familiar: more efficient institutions, enhanced powers for the European Parliament, a social policy, and the means to act decisively in the field of external relations. This was the basic recipe for Maastricht, which was known more correctly as the Treaty on European Union. With the signature of this treaty any remaining doubt about what a European Union might consist of was ended. The political nature of the transformation is underlined by making every national of a member state a citizen of the union with consequent rights and duties.

So this was the European Union. The European Economic Community was renamed simply the 'European Community' and remained the bedrock of the new Union, which was completed by the addition of some new areas of common endeavour among the members. Some of these, such as social policy, could be accommodated within the existing Community institutions. Others, in particular foreign policy, would be handled on an intergovernmental basis but still under the aegis of the Union. This made for a strange mixture of styles. On one hand, the fact that action is taken on behalf of a population enjoying full rights as citizens is reminiscent of a federation. This reading of the Union is, however, contradicted by its behaving as an alliance of sovereign states in its dealings with the outside world.

Naturally, therefore, the institution which bridges the gap between the routine workings of the Community and the higher ambitions of the Union is the European Council. Unashamedly intergovernmental, existing *de facto* from the mid 1970s, first appearing in a treaty as brief mention in the SEA, it is in the Treaty of Maastricht given a mission, which is to 'provide the Union with the necessary impetus for its development and ... define the general political guidelines thereof'. Acting as both a steering committee for further evolution and the engine room of the Union's foreign policy, the European Council was thus the link between a shared destiny and a recognizable identity. Its members would meet as politicians to discuss Europe and as Europeans to discuss politics.

The European Union established by Maastricht was therefore not quite as had been imagined by the Founding Fathers of European integration. In fact, the culmination of years of effort seemed to owe as much to Charles de Gaulle as to Jean Monnet. A quarter of a century since the Schuman Plan had held out the promise of a federal Europe, the supranational structures still remained underdeveloped. In contrast, the element of intergovernmentalism introduced as an afterthought was now the instrument through which Europe gazed both into its own navel and out to the wider horizons from where the world was looking back.

This, then, was the long-awaited European Union. Less than a federation, but with a vocation to make political sense of the commitment that member states of the Community had to each other. The question that was not answered was where exactly that was supposed to lead. During the negotiation of Maastricht, any reference to an eventual federation was ruled out by resistance from Britain in particular, with the result that refuge was taken in the vague aspirations expressed in the Treaty of Rome more than thirty years earlier. Maastricht therefore establishes a European Union which purports to be 'a new stage in the process of creating an ever closer union'. If clarity had been the guiding principle, the new Union could have either been proclaimed without further comment or with a statement that this was a step towards a federation. This is not the way that such matters are handled, however, and a form of words can usually be concocted to mean anything to anyone. The 'ever closer union' is a masterpiece of this style that has stood the test of time but, with a Union actually in place, it leaves the whole future of Europe hanging on the question of how close 'closer' can get.

We have seen that no satisfactory answer can be based simply on the operational characteristics of the European Union. Although interesting enough, a straight description of how routine business is conducted does not seem to explain how the paper and ink in circulation represents anything more than bureaucracy at its most arcane. Three institutions are interconnected by rules and procedures, some of which vary according to the matter in hand. Inside every institution are committees and working groups, each with its own task and its own methods. As in a great machine, the component elements go round and round, every one in its own space, each meshing with another, all part of the motion of the whole. Wheels within wheels turn in hidden corners, small movements produce larger ones, everything is order and energy. To the uninitiated, it is baffling, incomprehensible.

We can clarify things, however, by taking the analogy a little further to consider a motor car. Here is another assemblage of gears and cogs, cranks and pinions, all of which connect, engage and revolve in just the right order at precisely the right moment. This is a mechanic's perception in which shafts whirr and spin, pistons rise and fall, oil flows and electricity sparks. On the other hand, the same machine takes on a very different appearance from the point of view of the salesman. Now it becomes a style statement, a dream, an aspiration. From a grasp of the technical to a pursuit of the intangible, the understanding of what a car is thus changes dramatically in the eye of the beholder.

So it always has been with the European Union. From the very beginning the bits and pieces of its workings have to some people been the outward signs of a deeper fulfilment. A car, however, is not maintained by the salesman but by a mechanic. Once in the workshop, the verdict will not be that it has lost its sex-appeal but that there is a faulty fuel pump, or a blocked filter or something just as dull. Likewise, the European Union is capable of a more prosaic interpretation than that paraded by some of its enthusiasts. That is not to say that the spinners of dreams are wrong, but neither are the merchants of nuts and bolts. It is the relationship between the two which has driven European unification for half a century and which needs to be understood before anything useful can be said about the future.

**Theory and Practice**

There is nothing quite like the European Union. More than an international organization and less than a federation, it is a peculiar accumulation of principles and methods that is subject to evolution by fits and starts but always remains intact. The classic model of relations between states imagines their various interests as snooker balls that collide and rebound in complex interactions which have repercussions across the whole table. From this, in 1972 Andrew Shonfield developed an image of the Common Market as a bag of sticky marbles. This remains a nice description but does not provide an explanation of what is happening and how. Because of its constant development, a deep understanding of European integration calls for a theoretical framework that takes into account its dynamic nature. From this it follows that a theory of any value has to be predictive; more than just describing the current situation or presenting a vague hope it must say what will happen next and be proved right by events.

Early efforts in this respect were rooted in a body of theory known as functionalism, which was influential before the Second World War. This means that Monnet and his contemporaries were already aware of the very ideas that would be used to explain what they did; consequently there was at the outset an element of self-fulfilling prophesy in the way the subject was approached. There was also a weakness caused by taking a general theory of society and applying the same methods to a different sort of community. On the other hand, the theory had an obvious appeal in that it dealt with the way in which societies develop in relation the functions that are performed within them. The underlying assumption was that the Coal and Steel Community would become a European Federation in much the same way as a developed society grows from a primitive one.

Simply expressed, functionalism takes fundamental human needs such as food, shelter or companionship, and proposes that certain types of behaviour arose to satisfy these. From basic urges developed the institution of the family, followed by the household, the community, the tribe and the nation. Along the way these gave rise to 'derived needs' such as customs, rules, and eventually codified laws and political organization. Nobody set out purposely to develop these structures but they appeared as a result of the means employed to arrange things for survival, comfort and convenience. Thus as mankind as a whole goes from primitive to modern, more needs are provided for in cooperation, tasks become increasingly specialized and the group involved becomes more complex and more binding on the participants.

The parallel with international relations is tempting and was employed in the 1930s by David Mitrany as a model of how world peace could be achieved. Just as there came a point in evolution when humans no longer fought over the last scrap of dead antelope but worked together to obtain another carcass, Mitrany thought that war could be avoided in similar fashion. All that was required was to replace meat on the hoof with some modern essential such as coal or iron ore. Control of such resources traditionally depends on where they happen to be found, but functionalists would prefer to see authority over them allocated according to what they are needed for. Thus, function replaces sovereignty as the guiding principle of how things are organized and international jealousies give way to rational management by experts.

Mitrany drew inspiration from the example of such bodies as the Universal Postal Union established in 1874, by virtue of which it is possible to send mail anywhere in the world through the purchase of a stamp in the country of origin. A national Post Office does not need separate agreements with its counterparts in Poland, Egypt, Fiji and so on because all operate according to the rules of the Union. Likewise, the International Telecommunications Union of 1934, or the Civil Aviation Authority of 1945 deal with matters which are handled by specialists in the interests of all. In these instances there is a tension between technological progress and political structure that causes an overarching organization to come about naturally to fulfil an obvious need. These ideas chimed with a movement in architecture and design, typified by the Bauhaus school or the work of Le Corbusier, which took the view that form derives directly from purpose. Similarly, in the wider world, the dynamic of change at the heart of functionalism was thought to be 'technical self-determination'; in other words, the function determines the organization. Functionalists believed that the need of the modern world to tackle global themes such as pollution or raw materials would generate a range of appropriate organizations in an interconnected network overlying national sovereignties.

As a school of thought this was clearly attractive to the proponents of European integration, but in this context it shifted from being an explanation of how functions in *fact* shape society towards a belief in how functions *ought* to determine the principles on which international organizations are based. In this respect it rather resembled Marxism, which is both an ideology that aims to change the world and a theory which sets out why and how. Like Marxism it also looked to the day when the state would 'whither away'. Sympathizers were therefore *predicting* that the state would become irrelevant and also *calling for* this to happen. This was the intellectual atmosphere in which Jean Monnet and like minds were coming to grips with the economic and political situation in the aftermath of the Second World War. These key figures could be regarded as 'functional federalists'. Functionalism appealed to them as a mechanism for change and they then projected that forward to what they saw as its logical conclusion in a European Federation.

This explains to some extent why it was thought enough to start the ball rolling with the Schuman Plan and let the rest follow in due course. The problem was that there were two main flaws in the reasoning. Firstly, it ignored the fact that most functional needs could be provided for within an intergovernmental framework. Secondly, it assumed that an increase in shared problems would produce cooperation rather than conflict, which did not always prove to be the case. The possibility that the state would go quietly was disproved by the Empty Chair Crisis of 1965 which ensured that a Gaullian view of its importance would remain part of any further developments in Europe. Moreover, de Gaulle was not alone in his attachment to the state, which remained the primary focus of loyalty for many statesmen and ordinary people alike.

As things were not going as expected, a new theory called 'neo-functionalism' attempted to understand integration in the light of developments. This was most notably associated with Ernst Haas and essentially revolved around the idea of transnational relations between organized groups based in different countries. The parallel was then drawn with the pluralist view that in any single country the state exists to balance diverse interests one against the other. On this premise, Haas concluded that different transnational interests could only be reconciled by institutions above the state. The advantage of neo-functionalism was that it did not assume cooperation for the common good but allowed for the pursuit of selfish goals by a number of organized actors. It did presuppose a minimum existing bureaucracy equipped to address transnational interests and a background of public consensus or at least apathy so that nationalism did not enter the equation. The theory then envisaged that activity at the European level would increase through a process of 'spill-over', in which the integration of one sector leads to the integration of another in a sort of chain reaction.

Neo-functionalism as an academic theory went out of fashion when European integration entered the stagnation years of the 1970s. Nevertheless, it still seemed to explain some aspects of subsequent developments after the event and therefore enjoyed a revival in later years as political scientists attempted to produce an updated version. Ultimately, however, any hope of providing a viable conceptual framework must fade with every correction and adjustment introduced. As a starting point for discussion or a ready tool of analysis neo-functionalism still serves a useful purpose but is far from offering a holistic view of the processes that shape the European Union. Notably, it fails to deal adequately with the human element. In the early days this even involved a degree of wishful thinking as it was assumed that political spill-over would enable the Commission to become something like a European government. Certainly, some statesmen were ready to believe this and act accordingly until Charles de Gaulle determined that it was not going to be that sort of Europe. Conversely, when Margaret Thatcher and Jacques Delors took opposing views in the 1980s, the pace of progress towards the Frenchman's vision of Europe hardly faltered, but neither was there anything in neo-functionalist theory capable of foreseeing this outcome nor of adequately explaining it afterwards.

Of course, the effect of personalities is unpredictable but this fact is more than just another variable awaiting calculation; it exposes the fundamental weakness of a theory that says much about the interplay of interests and little about the concerns of people. While providing partial insights, it is rather like an understanding of forest management based on the knowledge of how a chain-saw works and what a tree is. In other words, it may be correct as far as it goes but is not generally helpful in application. Millions of citizens are unrepresented by organized interests but their hopes, fears and prejudices must surely count as important factors as Europe becomes more and more of a human community and less like the sterile political environment imagined by neo-functionalism.

Clearly there are watersheds in the integration of Europe that undermine any general law of incremental change and make it difficult to incorporate the defining moments in a comprehensive scheme of things. Jean Monnet imagined that functional forces of some sort might eventually bring about a European Federation, and since his day much intellectual effort has been expended in vain attempts fully to understand the mechanisms at work. After half a century, Europe is evidently not the same but what exactly is happening has always been something of a puzzle.

If political theory cannot bridge the gap between the awkward reality of European unification and our imperfect understanding of it, this deficiency itself may offer another way into the whole question. This means digging into the intellectual tool-kit for an item which has fallen rather out of fashion but seems curiously suited to the task. We shall look more closely into the history of European thought in the pages which follow, but at this point it is worth dwelling for a moment on the ideas of Auguste Comte, the early nineteenth century founder of positivism.

Comte postulated that human intelligence has three ways of coping with the unfathomable and tends to progress from one to the other in successive stages: theological, metaphysical, positive. In the first of these, things are explained by the presence of unseen influences, and in the second by abstract forces. In the third stage, however, the search for underlying causes is abandoned in favour of determining the relationship between specific phenomena. For example, the movement of the stars and planets was thought at one time to be the work of gods or other supernatural beings. Later it was imagined that some scientific principle must be in operation but nobody was sure what it might be. Finally, Isaac Newton asked himself why an apple fell to the ground and realized that what was true for the Earth and the fruit also applied to any two objects. The law of gravitation is therefore not primarily a statement of how the universe works but it does allow an accurate description of how solid bodies move relative to each other. Comte would see the cosmos as the sum of those relationships; once the equations are written, everything has been said.

The parallel with the way in which the subject of Europe has been approached is an interesting one. During the first (theological) stage it was thought that an innate sense of faith, honour and chivalry was the essence of a European brotherhood of the soul. In the second (metaphysical) stage came the search for an overarching theory to explain the untidy collection of institutions and practices that existed. If the comparison is continued, the third (positive) stage should replace the pursuit of a single truth with the correlation of observable effects. From this perspective Europe is not static but neither has it a particular driving mechanism any more than the solar system does. The movement of the planets may be imagined as clockwork, but there are no cogs and springs, only a relationship of one object to another based on size, speed and distance. Likewise, there is perhaps no 'Europe', only things that happen in a certain way according to laws of interaction that are known and understood.

The parallel between Comte's hypothesis and attitudes to European integration seems to be confirmed with the passage of time as intellectual efforts directed towards understanding the broad picture have largely given way to scrutiny of operational details. From the Single European Act onwards, a sea change has taken place in the range and depth of collective endeavour by the members of the Community but, even as treaty follows treaty, Europe remains defined more by how it works than by what it means. To apply Comte's method is therefore to conclude that the ultimate destiny of the European Union is a set of rules to cover a variety of activities in a number of circumstances.

If such is the future, there remains ample scope for change but it will be change in the sense of flexibility rather than evolution. In other words, Europe will be what it needs to be to do whatever it does but it will never be a federation. This runs counter to the view still held by those hoping for a federal union that the essential thing is to keep the project alive and await the day when it comes to fruition. Jacques Delors used to say that European integration was like riding a bicycle: you had to keep moving or fall off. While a clever turn of phrase for a mass audience, this image does not survive a moment's reflection even by a very occasional cyclist. Firstly, the rider may always apply the brakes and put his or her foot down. Secondly, any amount of pedalling does not substitute for knowing the way to the destination. For federalists, the prize is always at the end of the next rainbow and any effort vaguely in the right direction brings it a little nearer. It could be, however, that the Monnet method has reached its limit and that the remaining distance cannot be covered in sporadic forays as opportunity allows, no matter how much energy is expended.

Even if developments are federal in spirit it does not necessarily follow that they are an actual step in that direction. Without an explanation such as functionalism or its derivatives it is difficult to see how a series of reforms that have something of the federation about them will ever transform into the finished article. Even when theory was in its heyday it was least convincing with regard to how the final stage would be accomplished. The EU thus continues to hover between the community of sovereign states envisaged by Charles de Gaulle, and the federation promised by Jean Monnet. Neither is this an ambiguity that it is easy to adjust in favour of the latter conception through an accumulation of small touches. There is a qualitative difference between the two that sooner or later has to be addressed by an act of political will.

In the meantime, there is a sense in which the European Union works but is not finished. The big question is whether or not this matters. Early in this book the analogy was used of a construction site humming with activity but with nobody quite sure what was being built. To picture a single large scale civil engineering project being undertaken in this way requires a huge stretch of the imagination, but if the analogy is adapted slightly to cover a small town over a period of fifty years the scenario becomes more realistic. During half a century, building will have occurred intermittently when and where required. The first houses built are extended or have new roofs, a shopping centre replaces the old market, or a more modern railway station serves a larger population. Despite all this change, however, the town remains the sum of the things within it. These may not be quite the same as in days gone by but the purposes they serve and where they are in relation to each other define the space they occupy now as then. Materials and architecture move with the times but each cobblestone laid or every cubic metre of concrete poured is the consequence of a perceived need plus a few simple rules such as Building Regulations or the Town and Country Planning Act. Thus to outward appearances everything is different, while in reality the years have brought more of the same but in a variety of forms. The town is never 'finished' but at any moment it is complete.

Likewise, perhaps 'Europe' need never be more than whatever shape it takes at the time. Such a creation lacks the elegance of a grand design brought to fruition, but has the advantage of including a diversity of purpose within a workable system bringing tangible benefits.

## The European Mind

A matter-of-fact, pragmatic interpretation of the European Union certainly has the advantage of leaving aside any utopian flights of fancy. On the other hand, it does tend towards a denial of any underlying sense of belonging as a factor in past and future development. If the EU is essentially nothing more than what it provides, the only thing that unites us as Europeans is that we are all customers availing ourselves of the same service. Although such a no-nonsense view of Europe is clear and comprehensible, it does perhaps leave a niggling doubt that this is too sparse a description of a project encompassing the lives of millions of men and women.

There is even some evidence that a shared outlook on the social and cultural meaning of European citizenship is becoming engrained in the institutional checks and balances of the EU. In November 2004 the new President of the European Commission, José Manuel Barroso named the Italian politician Rocco Buttiglione as commissioner with responsibility for justice and fundamental freedoms. The problem was that Buttiglione was on record as saying that homosexuality was a sin and that the place of women was in the home. These extreme views provoked the European Parliament into threatening to block the investiture of the whole Commission if he were not replaced. Barroso backed down and a more acceptable candidate was put forward.

The point that Parliament was making is that some views are sufficiently 'un-European' to exclude anyone holding them from high office. This supposes that there are some ways of thinking which are more 'European' than others. It would, however, be hard to believe that Buttiglione is alone in his opinions.

The question therefore comes down to whether there is any particular thing in one European's head that makes him or her a kindred spirit for another European.

Of course, some features of an identifiably European culture are reasonably apparent. Certainly in the arts there is a shared heritage to which Europeans as a whole relate easily and naturally. Subject to personal taste, a symphony or an opera are appreciated in like manner in Rome or Berlin. Neither is this observation confined to classical music; it applies to the way in which music is understood and enjoyed in all its diversity. Jazz, blues and pop depend on the same harmonic structure and can be written in the same notation as the music of Beethoven or Berlioz. In the doh, ray, mi of the musical scale an entire people has ingrained within its collective consciousness the raw materials of everything from *Happy Birthday to You* to Mozart's *Requiem*. Of course individual tastes vary enormously and everyone has different preferences but, unlike the music of India or China for example, the whole repertoire is accessible to all Europeans in the same way. This means that, culturally, Europe extends beyond the EU, which has a short history compared to the creative community that has covered the continent for centuries. The Russian composers Tchaikovsky and Prokofiev both wrote scores for a ballet based on Romeo and Juliet, a play set in Italy written by an Englishman long dead. In fact European culture has spread even wider and has one of its most recognizable outposts in Sydney Opera House, half a world away from the land of Verdi and Rossini. It also takes in America, so that the United States and Russia have much in common on the cultural level. The salient point is that during the Cold War, the two superpowers were split not on cultural grounds but by ideological differences. The lesson is that a shared appreciation of the arts is not enough to form a cohesive European identity. More fundamental is a common outlook on how human lives should be ordered and the means by which this may be framed in a political context.

This is because the lessons that time has taught us are now engrained as a way of life. With the passing years have come accumulated habits of thinking that make us Europeans not only in our culture but in our politics. That shared journey of discovery is marked by three milestones; the Renaissance, the Reformation, and the Enlightenment.

At the end of fourteenth century the Renaissance heralded the end of the Middle Ages and the dawn of the modern world. This was a period of scientific advances, geographical discovery and a renewed interest in the writings of Greek and Roman times. Out of experiment, scholarship and adventure arose a new sense of individual human potential and a more active approach to the acquisition and application of knowledge as opposed to blind belief in dogma. Nevertheless, open deviation from official religious teachings normally brought retribution. The Polish astronomer Copernicus (1473-1543) postulated that the Earth and the other planets revolved around the Sun. This was regarded as heresy; according to the Church, God had made the universe with the Sun and stars all turning about the Earth. Unwilling to risk burning at the stake, Copernicus did not publish in his lifetime but left his writings to posterity. The Italian scientist Galileo (1564-1642) proved Copernicus correct but was summoned before the Inquisition and forced to bow to the doctrine that at the centre of every-thing the Earth was stationary. Legend has it that, rising from his knees at the end of his abjuration, he added 'But it does move!'. Galileo had done enough to keep himself out of the fire, but contained in his muttered defiance was the idea that all received wisdom was subject to question and every cause and institution open to challenge.

This was particularly relevant in the context of the Reformation, which began as an attempt to move the focus of attention in the Roman Catholic church away from obedience and towards faith. Change proved impossible and the Protestant movement emerged from 1517 as an alternative approach to personal salvation through Christ. Thus began a period during which national ambitions and religious forces became embroiled in over a century of bloodshed. The main concern of the Roman Church was to impose its authority over Christians everywhere. To this end it continued to operate through the secular state powers that carried out the pursuit and punishment of heretics. As time went by, however, states became reluctant to fulfil this role, not just because their rulers did not want to be subservient to the Pope, but because the constant strife made the business of running a country difficult. The need to allow for freedom of conscience thus led to a change in the nature of government. Where once the defining attribute of the state had been its capacity to impose conformity; now it had to be the guarantor of tolerance in order not to be torn apart.

Matters of conscience therefore impinged upon established traditions and touched upon questions about the ordering of society. Such questions were not new and the Renaissance had rediscovered the classical texts of antiquity on the subject. Thus stimulated, the minds of Europeans had already begun to approach politics as an exercise in organizing a large number of individual lives for practical purposes rather than to serve a system of belief. The Italian political philosopher Machiavelli (1469-1527) never attacked the dogma of the church but took a view of the state that was decidedly more worldly than religious and revolved around the effective use of power in furtherance of defined objectives. His was a state operating in its own interests rather than for the spiritual welfare of its citizens. The church did not enter into the question; what Machiavelli was considering was the political nature of statehood in the world as it then was.

At the other end of the scale, Michel de Montaigne (1533-1592) turned his attention to what it meant to be one man in that same world. Respected at the French court, Mayor of Bordeaux and a participant in the Wars of Religion, Montaigne was a privileged observer of his times but took as his theme the everyday business of life as he experienced it. Inventing the essay as a literary form, he handled the subject of what it was to be human by offering himself as an example and exploring his own feelings and outlook with candour and perception. Montaigne's work remains fresh to this day because he presents himself for the inspection of the reader not as a nobleman, nor as a Catholic, but as a person. He knows his station in life but chooses a standpoint based on curiosity and common humanity.

The importance attached to the exercise of understanding was also typical of the Dutch philosopher Spinoza (1632-1677) who with regard to politics concluded that: 'The monarchical form of government made an art of deceit by investing with the glamour of religion the awe on which the powerful rely to keep the masses in permanent subjection'. In England, Locke (1632-1704) published his own *Essay concerning Human Understanding* but also extended his thinking into the political sphere with *Two Treatises of Civil Government* in which he explored the idea of government by consent and described the fundamental importance of the legislative power. With Locke, Spinoza and others the idea was taking shape of a society organized on rational lines to accommodate the human mind in its individuality and to recognize the value of each.

This was the spirit of the Enlightenment: an eighteenth century philosophical movement which gave priority to reason and encouraged the reappraisal of existing ideas and institutions. Not that these surrendered everywhere to the new spirit of the age. An outspoken champion of religious, social and political liberty, Voltaire (1694-1778) endured several periods of banishment from his native France. In one respect this only added fuel to the flames, however, as Voltaire's exile in England made him familiar with the scientific work of Newton (1643-1727), which he popularized on his return. The cross-fertilization of English and French ideas continued in the political sphere when Montesquieu (1689-1755) was inspired by the work of Locke to publish his thoughts on legislation within the terms of a liberal constitution. There was little in *De l'Esprit des Lois* to shock later generations but at the time it was vehemently condemned by the church and placed on the Index, the list of forbidden books. While Montesquieu was defending his work, his fellow countryman Diderot (1713-1784) was in prison for producing a short book on blindness which in places seemed to undermine a standard proof for the existence of God based on the visible wonders of the natural world. Burnings at the stake had by now fallen into disuse but otherwise the power of the state was used much as in the time of Galileo to stifle any hint of independence of thought.

Subjected to official persecution, Diderot and Montesquieu were nevertheless sketching the outlines of the sort of regime founded on fair treatment and informed debate that would be a key feature of the accepted European model in years to come. Neither was a campaigning atheist nor an ardent democrat. They did not preach revolution and had little quarrel with the church or the monarchy as symbols but, like Spinoza, they despaired to see them combined at the head of a system rotten with ignorance and privilege. The alternative that they sought was a law-based state with rights for all. On this point many would have agreed, though the question may be approached in either of two ways. Diderot and Montesquieu would have said that an individual's rights derive from being a part of society in much the same way that membership of a club confers certain rights subject only to obeying the rules. The other way of looking at things is to say that any person has rights merely by virtue of being born and that society must be organized in such a way as to recognize these. That the purpose of government was to safeguard Man's natural rights was developed by the Swiss philosopher Rousseau (1712-1778), through whom it became an axiom of the French Revolution with the publication in 1789 of the *Declaration of the Rights of Man and of the Citizen*.

This text proclaimed that all men were born free and with the right to fair treatment and equality of consideration. Over the long and turbulent years that followed in Europe this guiding light never faded completely, so that the principles known as Human Rights eventually became the bench mark of respectability for political regimes everywhere. This was not merely a matter of yearning after some vague notion of a kinder world; on the other hand, neither was there a complete blueprint for Utopia. With the fine sentiments came basic rules for decent government that had developed to give practical expression to the idea that the individual is worthy of dignity and personal fulfilment.

These principles were codified in the European Convention on Human Rights signed in 1950, but the European Constitution of 2004 brought them for the first time into a document where they were given equal billing with transport policy, rules on budget deficits and all the details concerning the running of the EU machinery. After fifty years of claiming that Europe had a deeper significance it was probably not too soon to say what it meant besides quotas and tariffs. If there are certain truths that we hold to be self-evident, it is the function of a Constitution to state them for all to read.

Nobody in the EU today would want to see people oppressed by their rulers or tortured for their beliefs. On the other hand, opinion remains divided on the management of the economic forces to which they are subject. This debate also has its own history.

In the view of Marx (1818-1883) the coming of modern means of production merely changed one form of submission for another as 'for exploitation veiled by religious and political illusions it has substituted naked, shameless, direct, brutal exploitation'. Marx's answer of public ownership and state control was in contrast to the ideas of Adam Smith (1723-1790), who advocated free trade and private enterprise with minimum interference from government.

European thinking has long hovered between these two positions and, despite the fact that it was essentially economic in nature, the process of integration was launched without settling the question. There is therefore no fundamental principle underlying Europe in the economic field in the same way that Human Rights are the cornerstone of a system of political values, and this absence has allowed a shift of emphasis with the passage of time.

Jean Monnet is remembered as the father of the Community system but he was also an early guru of economic planning. Nothing outside of the communist bloc could have been more interventionist than the Coal and Steel Community, which was the free market tamed for political purposes. For the sake of peace and stability in western Europe, the normal interplay of comparative advantage was replaced by supranational control. The High Authority had powers to demand commercially sensitive information on such subjects as profitability or expansion plans. It could also co-ordinate investments, impose quotas, prevent unfair practices and take initiatives on the retraining of redundant workers or the creation of new jobs in alternative activities. In its basic conception and its operating methods, the Coal and Steel Community required that market forces give way to political will.

The opposite was true of the European Economic Community, where the object was not the imposition of controls but the removal of barriers in order to allow matters to be decided by competition. This reversal of policy represented a fundamental change in the way political action on a European scale was conceived. In 1950 the Schuman Plan proposed to override the operation of normal commercial relations on the grounds that it would be better all round to do so. In other words, commercial interests were made subservient to the general interest based on a political reading of what that might be. With the establishment of the Common Market, that was no longer the case unless it was assumed that what was best for business was best for everyone.

That position, although perfectly arguable, still does not have universal appeal. Of course nobody would expect the unemployed to starve, and social policies at national and EU level offer a range of palliatives to soften the effects of raw capitalism, but there is a view current in some circles that the European ethos should amount to more than the law of the jungle plus humane treatment for the casualties. The idea is that the EU should play a role in creating the conditions for a social market economy in which capital and labour can enjoy a mature and civilised relationship.

There is of course a balancing act in progress here which is part of the bigger picture of where Europe sits in relation to global economic forces. The question used to be easier when the world was divided into the two hostile camps of communism and capitalism. At the limits, the two models of society then on offer were based either on fear and ignorance or greed and stupidity. As members of the 'West', countries of what was then the European Economic Community tended to lean rather towards the latter. In the post-Cold War world that choice is not always accepted as natural in quite the same way and there is a feeling in some circles that the European Union should provide a safe haven from the globalisation of unrestrained consumerism.

This view accepts that in the world today politics and economics go together on a grand scale. Recognising that reality, it regards the EU as the means by which ordinary people can be put back into the equation. What is at issue is the sort of society that the European project implies in a wider sense and how that conception relates to the systems in place. Again, it is a question of who we think we are and what we want to do about it.

# 5: EUROPE FOR EVERYONE

## Convention and Constitution

If building a warm-blooded Europe of life and energy means putting people back into politics, the political process must be open and meaningful. Already, everyone has the opportunity to vote in elections for the European Parliament. As far as most of us are concerned, however, it is as if we were voting for the high priesthood on the Planet of the Robots. Whatever we do in the local polling station, in Brussels the wheels turn mysteriously and the machine clanks out the rhythm to which we eat and drink, work and play. We are organised but not engaged. Between our human lives and the world of the Eurocrats is a fog of incomprehension which we are not encouraged to penetrate.

A large part of the problem is that the European project has gradually become bogged down in petty detail as one treaty follows another and each consists of a list of amendments to the previous one article by article, all referred to by number. For example, the Treaty of Nice (2001) states that 'In Article 159, the third paragraph shall be replaced by the following…'. This is meaningless unless the reader actually turns up Article 159 in the Treaty of Amsterdam, which then refers back to Article 130b of Maastricht. In some instances the paper trail leads back to the Treaty of Rome (1957) or, rarely nowadays, to the Treaty of Paris (1951) which established the Coal and Steel Community. To the layman the whole thing is completely impenetrable.

At the start of the twenty-first century the European Union was preparing to enlarge to twenty-five members, all subject to the same layers of gobbledegook that had built up over the years. The idea gained ground that it was time to start again with the preparation of a new text that would be both workable and transparent. This was all very well, but in the EU things rarely happen merely because it would be a good idea. Time and again, action is taken because circumstances either demand it or provide the opportunity for decisive intervention by groups or individuals who want it. Often it is both.

The story of the European Constitution begins in 1992 with the Treaty of Maastricht. This took the major step of establishing the European Union but recognised that a certain amount of tidying up would be required at a later date. The text therefore stated that an intergovernmental conference (IGC) would be convened in 1996 to decide what new measures to take.

From this came the Treaty of Amsterdam 1997, which did a good deal of generally useful tinkering but failed to address an issue which would later become urgent. This problem was a particularly sticky one because it left absolutely no scope for any sort of fudge relying on the creative use of words; it was a matter of numbers.

Firstly, the number of Commissioners needed to be reduced. With fifteen countries in the EU, the five largest each nominated two Commissioners, while the rest were entitled to one each, making a total of twenty. This was already more than enough, but the addition of new members from all of the joining countries would definitely make the Commission too large and unwieldy. Even if the big five gave up their extra nominees, there would still be too many at twenty-five members. Ideally, the Commission should be fewer in number than the list of countries in the Union. In principle, the fact that some countries would no longer have 'their' men and women round the table would make no difference because all Commissioners are independent and act in the greater interests of Europe as a whole. In practice, the idea was a hard one to swallow.

The second point of difficulty was in regard to the system of voting in the Council of Ministers. Where unanimity was still the rule there was no problem: if everyone said 'Yes', the matter was decided. These cases were becoming rarer, however, as more and more subjects were dealt with by qualified majority vote (QMV). This meant that if a proposal obtained enough votes it was passed, but the votes of some countries were worth more than others. For example, a raised hand from the British minister was counted as ten votes, whereas that of the Belgian was be five, or the Irish member only three. These weightings were arranged so that a 'blocking majority' to reject a proposal was in the hands of the large countries. Ten new members would change the mix dramatically and require a rebalancing of the figures.

With regard to both the size of the Commission and the mathematics of the Council of Ministers, the Treaty of Amsterdam (1997) failed to grasp the nettle and left the problem for another day. The next opportunity came in the latter half of 2000, when a new intergovernmental conference was held to prepare the ground for a new treaty. The IGC culminated in a full summit meeting in the town of Nice, where the leaders of the fifteen countries were to iron out any final points before signing the finished document. Unfortunately, this summit was remarkable mainly for its shambolic organisation by a French presidency made impotent by internal rivalry. As a result, the Treaty of Nice was a sorry mish-mash of whatever the participants could bear to see included.

Worst of all, the recalculation of the weighted votes in a logical manner was made impossible by the refusal of France to accept fewer votes than Germany. From the Schuman Plan onwards, the two countries had always enjoyed equal ranking in this respect but, after reunification, the sheer size of Germany called for at least a gesture that would reflect the new reality. French intransigence prevented this and so the question was not dealt with on a rational basis. The figures arrived at, country by country, were: Germany 29, UK 29, France 29, Italy 29, Spain 27, Poland 27, Netherlands 13, Greece 12, Czech Republic 12, Belgium 12, Hungary 12, Portugal 12, Sweden 10, Austria 10, Slovakia 7, Denmark 7, Finland 7, Ireland 7, Lithuania 7, Latvia 4, Slovenia 4, Estonia 4, Cyprus 4, Luxembourg 4, Malta 3.

This satisfied France, but at the price of giving Spain and Poland an inflated status. These two countries with a combined population of 80 million had 54 votes between them, compared to Germany's 29 votes for the same population. Moreover, Germany was a net contributor to the EU budget, whereas Poland was due to join Spain as a beneficiary. Nevertheless, the Treaty of Nice had to be signed because it provided a bare minimum framework for enlargement of the EU. In other respects it was a shoddy piece of work cobbled together in desperation and would some day have to be put right. This was the real impetus for starting afresh with a new text that would rationalise the whole system from scratch and, incidentally, make sense of it all for the average citizen.

This task was entrusted to Valéry Giscard d'Estaing, the former President of France who had taken a leading role in the development of the European Economic Community on the 1970s. In February 2002 Giscard convened a Convention bringing together representatives from the existing member states, the candidate states, the European Parliament and national parliaments. The resulting Draft Constitution for Europe was presented to the leaders of the twenty-five countries at the EU summit in July 2003. After a good deal of heated discussion a final version was signed in October 2004. At the time of writing it still awaits ratification by most of the signatory states: a process that requires a referendum in some cases.

On the subject of the institutions of the EU, the Constitution goes a fair way to correcting the deficiencies of the Treaty of Nice.

In this respect, it replaces the system of weighted voting in the Council of Ministers by a 'double majority'. This means that, for most items on the agenda, a decision goes through if it is approved by at least 55% of the member states representing at least 65% of the population of the EU. In addition, a blocking majority must consist of at least four countries. On the question of the size of the Commission, this will be capped at two-thirds of the number of member states with effect from the year 2014.

In addition to these and related matters of an essentially arithmetic nature, the Constitution contains two important institutional innovations:

1) The EU is to have a Minister for Foreign Affairs, appointed by the European Council. He or she will conduct the Common Foreign and Security Policy and also serve as Vice-President of the Commission.

2) The system whereby the functions of the EU presidency are taken over every six months by a different country in rotation will be replaced by a permanent post for one person. This position will in future be occupied by an individual elected by the European Council for two and a half years, with the possibility of reappointment after this period.

Other changes to the EU institutions reaffirm the role of the Commission and give a higher profile to the European Parliament. The overall effect of the Constitution has been to tidy up a piecemeal collection of treaty provisions and working practices which had become outdated, dysfunctional and obscure. In this respect it has been something like the defragmentation program on a computer which consolidates all the clutter scattered here and there on the hard disk over time.

Nobody could deny the job of 'tidying-up' done by the new Constitution. However, the suspicion of those who are not in any case well disposed towards the European Union is that this is not just innocent rationalisation but the preparatory work for a European 'superstate' of a more federal character. In fact it could be both or either; European integration was ever thus. It is more than thirty years since Andrew Shonfield famously described the process as a 'journey to an unknown destination' and we are not much wiser now. There is still no master plan. Today, as it was in the beginning, results on the ground reflect an unspoken pact between Technicians and Dreamers. Under the influence of this odd couple, our Europe has become an accumulation of odds and ends that is a rich field of study for the historian, but which defies satisfactory explanation in the here-and-now. The Constitution is in this sense an attempt to sweep away the cobwebs of more that half a century to speak to the present age. If it does not tell us where we are going, at least it says where we are at the moment.

This still leaves open the questions of who **we** are and what we want next. On the legal and administrative level, the Constitution is a decent piece of clerical work but its writers had more trouble in explaining what the European Union means in human terms because of divergencies of view on the subject.

Although the chapter on social policy is replete with fine sentiments, it fails to set out a standard view of what it means to be a member of a society in which people work for money. To some extent, there are historic and cultural reasons for this. The tendency on the Continent is to see capital and labour as 'social partners', with accepted responsibilities on both sides. This contrasts with the traditional British attitude that workers and management are class enemies. The text also has to paper over differences between those countries which have strong legislation governing how workers are hired and fired and those where flexibility in the labour market is seen as an asset. Torn between being too prescriptive and too liberal, the Constitution falls back on the device of finding a form of words which offends as few sections of opinion as possible. Perhaps this is understandable but it does detract from any overarching vision of life in the modern world as seen from the EU.

The writers of the Constitution did nevertheless try hard to put the economic and legal aspects of the EU into a broader context by setting out the human values that the whole administrative edifice is supposed to embody. The obvious temptation was to fall back on the Christian heritage that had inspired Coudenhove-Kalergi and had later provided much of the moral underpinning for post-war European integration. This was resisted during the drafting of the Constitution, but pressure continued from some of the large predominantly Catholic countries to have a reference inserted in the signed version. The arguments against generally revolved around the fact that Europe is an ethnically diverse society and to claim an exclusively Christian foundation for its spiritual meaning would be divisive and even offensive. This argument was valid on practical grounds and it was certainly fair to deploy it but there are two other good reasons for not attaching the EU to any particular system of belief. Firstly, there are elements of European culture which are purely secular. Secondly, many of the social and political instincts which Europeans now accept as normal were in fact formed through long years of opposition to organised religion.

The preamble to the Constitution therefore had to walk a tightrope between the religious faith which had been the very essence of Europe for centuries and the, equally European, legacy of rationalism and tolerance from the Enlightenment. Explicit references to Christ and God did not make it to the draft stage but 'respect for reason' was only weeded out just before the final version was signed.

The form of words which actually appears is thus:

> DRAWING INSPIRATION from the cultural, religious and humanist inheritance of Europe, from which have developed the universal values of the inviolable and inalienable rights of the human person, freedom, democracy, equality and the rule of law...
>
> BELIEVING that Europe, reunited after bitter experiences, intends to continue along the path of civilisation, progress and prosperity...

Behind the agonised finesse of the drafting, this statement boils down to something like: 'As Europeans, we now understand that we can have religion without burning people at the stake, and that we can have technology without raining down high explosives on each other'. If that is the basic message of the European Union, it can only be applauded.

History has made Europe what it is. If we all learn the same lesson from our long years together, we at least have that much in common. On the sixtieth anniversary of the liberation of the extermination camp at Auschwitz, the President of France, Jacques Chirac, made a speech in which he described a Europe united by the memory of past tragedies and committed to stamping out hatred, intolerance and fanaticism in future.

No sane person would deny that this is progress. Within the last sixty years we have decided that Europeans will never again take millions of innocent men, women and children and gas them like vermin. Very good. The question which concerns us here, however, is whether or not we need the European Union to be the guardian of our collective memory. Have we not in any case put such barbarity behind us? Is a Constitution which purports to guarantee basic human decency: 1) unnecessary and, 2) out of place in an organisation which fulfils a primarily economic purpose.

Jean Monnet used to say that men come and go but only institutions grow wiser. Whether or not we agree is the key to whether or not we believe in the sort of European Union that needs a Constitution.

## The Day after Tomorrow

Any sense of identity that a unified Europe might derive from a broader vision of its purpose has always been subject to circumstances. As times have changed, so has any meaning that it has been possible reasonably to attach to its construction. Even as a new Europe could be glimpsed in the origins of the Coal and Steel Community, the idea that this might be a community of Christian souls was incongruous. Not that this conception was very different from the common humanity which demanded an end to the Franco-German rivalry which had been the cause of so much bloodshed. From this reconciliation came a group of countries committed to a sort of unity different to that of the totalitarian East: a foothold for freedom on this side of the Atlantic.

There has therefore always been a sort of European self-awareness vaguely glimpsed in a sense of mission, but it is now the first decade of a new millennium and the old references no longer apply. Europe today is a multicultural society of which the Christian religion can no longer claim to be the bedrock. France and Germany will never again go to war against each other and drag in neighbouring countries and perhaps the whole world. The Cold War is over and the East/West divide is a memory from another age. So what greater role does the European Union fulfil for the mass of humanity it embraces and what does it promise for the future?

For many years the issue of exactly what sort of Europe was being built was lost in a conspiracy of silence between those who had no interest in asking the question and those who dared not give an answer. In the meantime, more and more bits and pieces have been added to the structure. The result is an imposing edifice, a monument to ingenuity and perseverance upon which millions of ordinary men and women can only gaze in wonder. But what is it for? The short answer must be that it is for us. That only leaves one question: what sort of Europe do we want?

One thing is certain. Because Europeans are political creatures, a community of hearts and minds can only be one in which citizens are politically engaged. Just as surely, this can not be achieved by applying a touch here and there to sketch the semblance of a federation in the hope that one day it will become the real thing. After half a century there are still no obvious forces in play capable of producing such a transformation of themselves. The change from a Europe of ways and means to a Europe of people and ideas is not as inevitable as once it seemed. Rather than a destiny to be fulfilled, it is now an option to be considered; rather than a mystery to be understood, it is now a job to be tackled.